WITHDRA

D0015842

John,

Live Your Values

Best

Mark Erwin

11/5/04

"As one of the financial industries' most valuable resources, Bill Bachrach has contributed an inestimable amount to the skills, esteem, and credibility of the financial professional. **Now he's unveiled the secrets of top advisors and made their most important and effective tools available to everyone, including do-it-yourselfers and clients of financial companies everywhere.** This will undoubtedly boost the business of excellent advisors and help to 'raise the bar' for anyone who is not yet serving clients in a way that really matters."

    —Jonathan Steinberg, CEO of Individual Investor Group, Inc.

"*Values-Based Financial Planning* breaks through the primary reason for not achieving financial success: procrastination. Procrastination can be defined as knowing what you *should* do but not knowing *why you want* to do it. By taking an easy, step-by-step approach to setting *non*-financial goals, it quickly establishes the basis for a meaningful financial plan. Bill's uniquely positive method is fun, inspirational and a surefire way to make certain the plan is implemented successfully."

    —John Wheat, president of
    Successful Money Management Seminars

"If all Bill Bachrach gave us in *Values-Based Financial Planning* was his sound, practical, step-by-step process for creating a Financial Road Map™, this book would be well worth our time. He gives much more, however, in his counsel on finding a Trusted Advisor® as opposed to a salesperson. **I recommend Bill's book to everyone who wants to gain control over their finances and become financially healthy.**"

    —Hyrum W. Smith, Vice-chair of the Franklin Covey Co.

"From our experience of working with more than five thousand entrepreneurs over the past twenty-five years, we know that highly successful people want a coach they trust to provide them with direction and confidence. *Values-Based Financial Planning* helps you create a Financial Road Map that lays out the financial future. Bill starts with a simple premise: what's truly important to you in all areas of your life. **With a clear understanding of your fundamental life values, the best possible financial plan and strategies emerge.**"

—Dan Sullivan and Babs Smith,
creators of The Strategic Coach®

"By the time you finish reading this book, you will have created a Financial Road Map to serve as your personal guide, as well as discovered your core values and what is necessary to achieve your goals. **Anyone who cares about his or her financial future should read this book.** Whether you have a financial professional or prefer to do it yourself, you will be inspired."

—Howard Kaloogian,
Member of the California State Legislature

VALUES-
BASED
FINANCIAL
PLANNING™

The Art of
Creating
an Inspiring
Financial
Strategy

VALUES-
BASED
FINANCIAL
PLANNING™

The *Art* *of*
Creating
an Inspiring
Financial
Strategy

BILL BACHRACH

Aim High Publishing
San Diego, California

Aim High Publishing
8380 Miramar Mall, Suite 200
San Diego, CA 92121

Copyright © 2000 by Bill Bachrach

All rights reserved, including the right of reproduction in whole or in part in any form.

First edition 2000
Eleventh printing 2004

Designed and typeset by Robert Mott & Associates • Keswick, Virginia
Illustrated by Tom Klare • San Diego, California
Edited by Just Write • Keswick, Virginia
Printed in the United States of America
ISBN: 1-887006-03-6

This book is designed to provide accurate and authoritative information on the subject of personal finances. It is sold with the understanding that neither the author nor the publisher are engaged in rendering legal, accounting, or other professional services by publishing this book. As each individual situation is unique, questions relevant to personal finances and specific to the individual should be addressed to an appropriate professional to ensure that the situation has been evaluated carefully and appropriately. The author and publisher specifically disclaim any liability, loss, or risk which is incurred as a consequence, directly or indirectly, of the use and application of any of the contents of this work.

OTHER BOOKS BY BILL BACHRACH

Values-Based Selling: The Art of Building High-Trust Client Relationships for Financial Advisors, Insurance Agents and Investment Reps

High-Trust Leadership: A Proven System for Developing an Organization of High-Performance Financial Professionals (with Norman Levine)

Trademarked Words

The following terms in this book are trademarked by Bachrach & Associates, Inc: Financial Road Map, Four Quadrants, Quality of Life Enhancer Worksheet, Values-Based Financial Plan, Values-Based Financial Planning, Values Conversation, and Values Staircase.

I dedicate this book to the Trusted Advisors,
who work hard every day to
help people align their financial choices
with their core values so they can
have a better quality of life.

ACKNOWLEDGEMENTS

Special thanks to the following individuals who assisted with the completion of this book:

My wife, Anne, whose contributions always result in a better finished product.

Karen Risch for doing all the hard work it takes to make a book like this sensible for and sensitive to the reader.

Robert Mott and Tom Klare for making it look great with dynamic design and fun illustrations.

Kathryn K. Ioannides, Director of Education and Examination for the Certified Financial Planner Board, for her insights and detailed explanation about the requirements for the CFP designation.

Those who reviewed the manuscript prior to publication, including Anne Bachrach, Theresa Biggerstaff, Jim Cathcart, Layne Cutright, Chuck Ebersole, Gail Fink, John Hansch, Tom Hansch, Deborah and Sidney Haygood, Sharon Petro, Floyd Shilanski, Catherine Spear, and Mark Van Leeuwen.

The Trusted Advisors who helped us collect comments from their clients for inclusion in this book, including Rod Carson, George Meyerhoff, Sybil Praski, David Stone, Floyd Shilanski, and Mark Van Leeuwen.

CONTENTS

INTRODUCTION

In the grand scheme of things, money's not that important. It's significant only to the extent that it allows you to enjoy what is important to you. And *not worrying* about your finances is critical to having a life that excites you, nurtures those you love, and fulfills your highest aspirations.

Values-Based Financial Planning™ will help you build a financial strategy, starting with your unique values. Defining them will help you create a plan that not only looks good on paper but also spurs you to follow through. If you have a future, and most of us do, regardless of age or net worth, this book will help you realize what's important to you, align your financial choices with the great life you want, and become inspired to do whatever it takes to have that life.

Every great accomplishment has a sound strategy behind it, and creating the financial future you desire is no different.

Spontaneity definitely spices up your life, but having no plan is a recipe for mediocrity. What if the Egyptians had winged it when building the pyramids? Or if the astronauts had known only generally where they were headed? Great feats are achieved as a result of people simply knowing what they want and why! Athletes attain Olympic glory; musicians perform at Carnegie Hall; scientists, writers, philanthropists, and politicians earn the Nobel Prize. And many people who'll never make headlines create the good life for themselves—as they define it—and greatly reduce or eliminate their financial stress. This is what *Values-Based Financial Planning* is already doing for the clients of top-drawer financial professionals. This is what it can do for you.

What would *your* life be like if you had a financial strategy based on what was truly important to you, where your investments and insurance programs were working in harmony to achieve your goals? This would be in stark contrast to what most people have, which is a hodgepodge of financial products purchased one by one over the years from various salespeople and companies, based on tips from friends or information in brochures.

Many people wind up reacting to events rather than designing and implementing a financial plan.

As much as approaching finances strategically sounds like common sense, most people wind up buying a little insurance here, a few stocks there, and funding some kind of retirement plan to be safe. They buy to meet needs, which may be real or the product of media hype. They, like most of us, were probably pressured by an indelicate reminder that they, too, will die someday—maybe sooner than they think.

I started out in the sales game, so I know how it's played, and I know the limitations of buying financial products from salespeople. Now I'm in a related but very different kind of career: Since 1988, I've acted as coach and consultant to some of the most effective, best producers with investment, financial planning, and insurance companies, helping them help their clients make smart choices about money. My business today is coaching financial professionals not to be salespeople but instead Trusted Advisors®—both a term I've coined and a descriptive title for those I train. Nowadays, my profession is more about process than products. This works to your benefit: You'll learn how the uppermost echelons of financial services operate—and how you can get the same benefits as their lucky clients by using what this book has to offer.

This is the first time I have shared this information with the general public. It's my goal for you to use it in laying the foundation for a completely doable plan to lead you into an inspiring financial future. The good news is that it's never too late; *now* is always a good time to get started.

Whether you want to enlist a professional's help or go it alone, by the time you finish reading and complete the exercises in each section's checklist, you will have clarified your values (chapter 1), accurately prioritized and precisely defined your goals (chapter 2), and benchmarked your current financial reality (chapter 3). You will also have created a Financial Road Map® (chapter 4) to serve as your guide in implementing your plan.

Taking care of your money is simple: time consuming, but simple. For some it can be a hassle, bore, or distraction from what's really important to them. If you think you might like to delegate the management of your investments, insurance, and other financial vehicles, chapter 5 will help you decide if this approach is right for you. Then you can use chapters 6 and 7 to find a competent professional to complete and carry out your financial plan. You'll learn the inside story on the financial services industry and how to recognize a trustworthy financial advisor, as well as what you should expect in a working relationship with this person.

Yet if you choose to do it yourself, this book will help you base your financial decisions on what's important to you—not a hot tip, the latest bestseller, your friends' recommendations, or someone you see on TV. Do-it-yourselfers will have to be adept at math, learn to factor rates of inflation relevant to specific goals, and become educated about types of investments and insurance. Chapter 5 will guide you to the proper resources.

Values-Based Financial Planning will not offer you get-rich-quick tips, nor will it explain the rudiments of insurance and investments. It will not tell you where or why to buy life insurance or how or when to sell your stocks. It will not warn you about the possible collapse of Social Security or alert you to the shifting paradigms in corporate America that necessitate more personal financial planning. It's simply not that kind of book.

Nor will it instruct you in how to create and implement a financial plan from beginning to end, but it will tell you the best way to start. This book is about taking control of the financial planning *process*—and of the financial plan only if that's what you really want. It will not advocate doing it yourself, nor will it chastise you for wanting to do it that way. This book is about finding your own way. This book is about *you.*

You might already be wealthy. Then again, you might not. You obviously have an interest in money and planning for the future. You either attended a Values-Based Financial Planning seminar, were given this book by a caring friend or an expert you've consulted, or you had the personal fortitude to march into a bookstore (or to type in the URL of an online book source) and plunk down your hard-earned cash for grist in your financial mill. Regardless of your financial stature, plans for the future, or current level of fiscal sophistication, this book will help you make smart choices about your money, and I'm honored to make a small contribution to your success.

SECTION 1

"WHAT ARE THE FIRST STEPS IN PLANNING FOR MY FUTURE?"

With the first four chapters of this book, you will take specific actions to lay the groundwork for your financial plan. You will discover your core values and how they relate to your financial goals, benchmark your current financial situation, and begin to create a visual representation of all that's important to you in realizing your plans for a secure and prosperous future. As you complete each exercise, check it off in the list on the next page. You'll notice that the gratification and momentum you get from finishing these manageable tasks will help propel you through the book and on to implementing your customized Values-Based Financial Plan™.

SECTION 1 CHECKLIST

✔ Date Completed

_____

❑ _____ Conduct the Values Conversation™ with a partner.

❑ _____ Complete the goals worksheet.

❑ _____ Collect and organize your financial information.

❑ _____ Create a Financial Road Map.

"We found the Values-Based Financial Planning process to be very helpful in preparing our financial plan. It helped us carefully plan for the future and then develop a strategy that reflects our goals and values. With confidence in the process, it is much easier to remain committed to our plan and make good choices for the future."

Bernie and Randy Schwartz
Pharmacists • Saskatchewan, Canada

"The conversation about our values and completing the whole road-map process allowed us to more clearly understand our priorities so that we are motivated to stay on track to accomplish what we want for our future."

Darwin and Janette Benedict
Field Data Inspector and Teacher • Denver, Colorado

CHAPTER 1

BASE YOUR PLAN ON WHAT'S IMPORTANT TO YOU: DEFINING YOUR VALUES

*Self-reflection
is the school of wisdom.*

BALTASAR GRACIÁN,
The Art of Worldly Wisdom (1647)

If you were to consult the best financial advisors on how to plan for your future, they wouldn't start by educating you about market trends or mortality. They wouldn't try to explain the pros and cons of mutual funds, insurance, or any other financial vehicles. And they certainly wouldn't bore you with their resumes.

Instead, they'd focus on what's important to you. They'd focus on your values.

This word, *values*, gets knocked around a good deal nowadays. Everyone from the far right to the extreme left has planted a flag on the term to claim it as their own. Just what are values, anyway? For our purposes, we'll define them in a broad sweep: *Values are those qualities and principles intrinsically valuable or desirable to you.* That means they have particular significance—the words *you* use to describe them give you an emotional high, and their fulfillment is what your life is really all about. *They are life's emotional payoff.* Politics and pop psychology aside, values are also the bedrock of sound financial planning.

Most financial planning starts with an assessment of goals. Important as these are, they don't provide you with the big picture, the "why" behind the rest of the plan, your *values.* Goals are the tangible results you seek, while values are the intangibles that make pursuit of those goals genuinely meaningful to you.

The Values Conversation you'll learn in this chapter was designed to be used by high-level financial professionals to work with their best clients. But there's no reason you can't do this simple process at home with a partner. It reveals your core values, which make any resulting plan have more personal meaning and therefore move you to action more effectively than anything else. It also facilitates accurate goal prioritization, which you'll complete in chapter 2, "Make Meaningful Milestones: Setting Worthwhile Goals."

If you are already working with a financial advisor and you want to include him or her in your progress through this book, this would be a good exercise to share. Or you can complete it just as successfully with a spouse, parent, friend, or even a mature child. All you need are page 17, a pen or pencil, your partner, and the right attitude.

Approach this exercise with a sense of curiosity and willingness to learn about what makes your life meaningful to you.

HERE'S HOW THE VALUES CONVERSATION WORKS

1. Your partner asks you a simple question: "What's important about money *to you?*"

2. Your job is easy: Just answer truthfully. Take as much time as you need, and give the first answer that comes to mind.

3. Your partner records your answer on the bottom step of the Values Staircase™ (see example on page 6).

4. Then your partner builds on your answer by asking another question, substituting your value for the word *money:* "What's important about [your last answer] *to you?*"

5. Again you respond with your first thought, your partner records it, and then he or she asks you the question again: "What's important about [the value you just said] *to you?*" And so on, up the staircase.

We stress "to you" because money, like values, means different things to different people. Some pursue it for security, others for freedom, still others for something entirely different. Yet all values move us at our deepest levels because they are pure, undiluted emotions. Consider the emotional power of values such as *independence, pride, providing for family, accomplishment, achievement, balance, making a difference, fulfillment, spiritual attainment, inner peace,* and *self-worth.* These are only a few examples of the values you may consider important. Your core values may comprise a completely different list. Of course, there are no wrong answers. *Your* answer is the right one.

In the sample Values Conversation below, Terry is just starting the financial planning process and a friend, Dale, is helping by acting as facilitator. As you read their conversation, notice how Dale writes Terry's answers from the bottom to the top of the Values Staircase™.

Dale.   Okay, let's get started. **What's important about money *to you*?**

Terry.   Well, money gives me security.

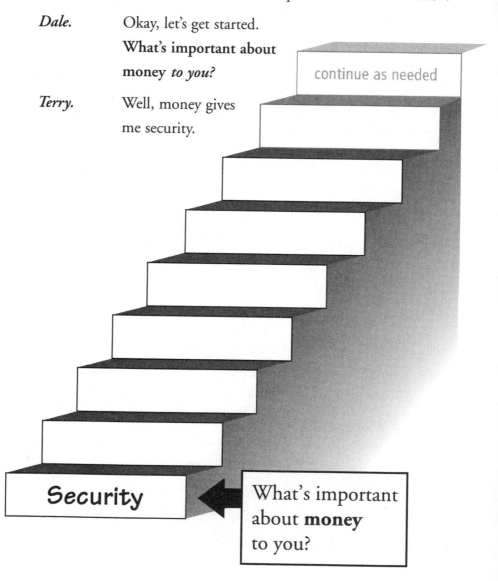

continue as needed

Security

What's important about **money** to you?

Dale. *[After writing **security** on the bottom step, Dale continues.]* What's important about security *to you?*

Terry. Having security allows me to do what I want to do, when I want to do it. I feel a sense of freedom.

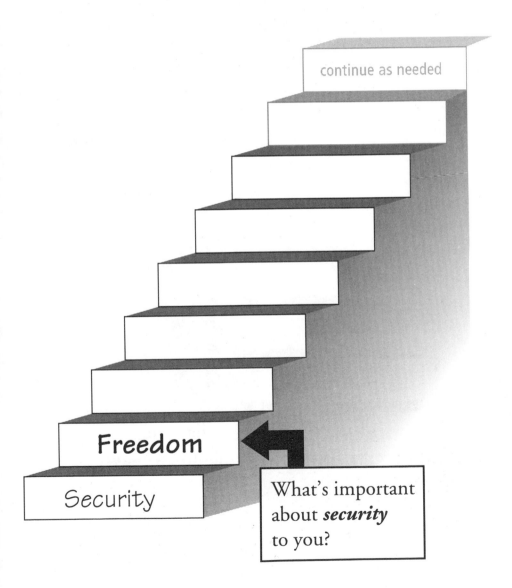

continue as needed

Freedom

Security

What's important about **security** to you?

Dale. *[After writing* **freedom** *on the second step, Dale continues.]* What's important about freedom *to you?*

Terry. With freedom, I have more time to be with my family.

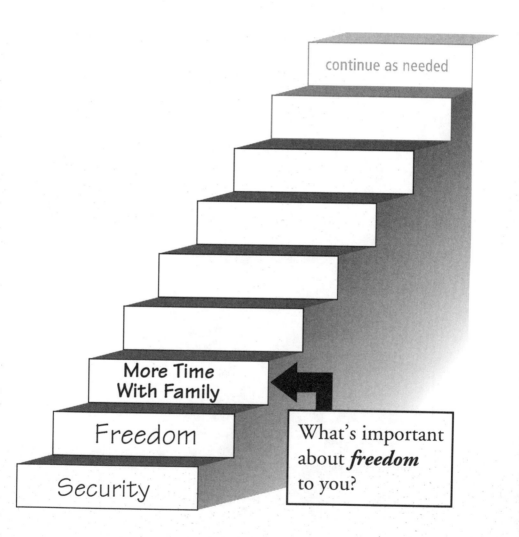

Dale. [*After writing* **more time with family** *on the third step, Dale continues.*] What's important about having more time with your family *to you?*

Terry. I can enjoy more balance in my life.

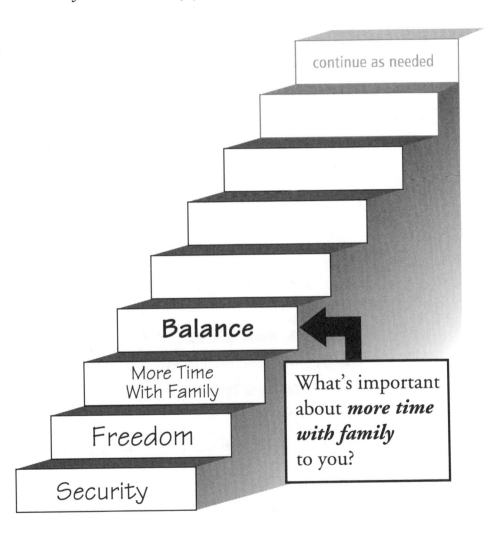

continue as needed

Balance

More Time
With Family

Freedom

Security

What's important
about ***more time
with family***
to you?

Dale. *[After writing* **balance** *on the next step, Dale continues.]* What's important about enjoying balance *to you?*

Terry. I don't really have that right now. Uh . . . Let's see. If I did have more balance in my life, I would feel a great sense of accomplishment.

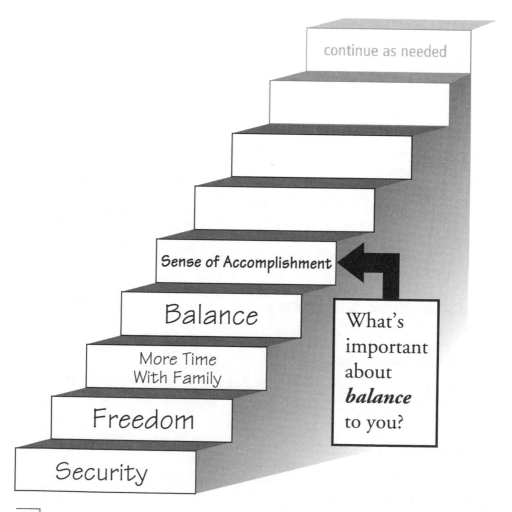

Dale. [*After writing* **sense of accomplishment** *on the next step, Dale continues.*] What's important about a sense of accomplishment *to you?*

Terry. Wow, that's tough to answer.

Dale. [*Staying <u>silent</u> while Terry considers the answer.*]

Terry. I guess that accomplishment allows me to make a difference in other people's lives. And what's important about that is I can be the best I can be.

continue as needed

Terry gave two answers at once, so each gets written on its own step.

Being the Best I Can Be

Make a Difference in Other People's Lives

Sense of Accomplishment

Balance

More Time With Family

Freedom

Security

What's important about *a sense of accomplishment* to you?

Dale.   [*After writing* **make a difference in other people's lives** and **being the best I can be** *on the next two steps, Dale continues.*] Now what's important about making a difference in other people's lives and being the best you can be *to you?*

Terry.   Well, that's really what life is all about to me. It makes me feel like my life really has purpose.

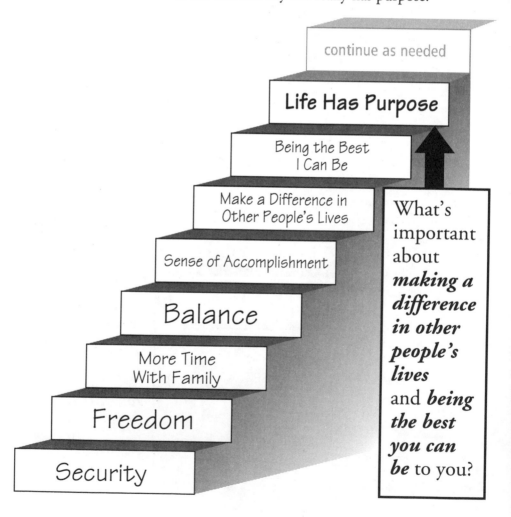

Dale.   *[After writing* **life has purpose** *on the next step, Dale continues.]* What's important about your life having purpose *to you?*

Terry.   I don't think there's anything more important to me than that. I think that's it.

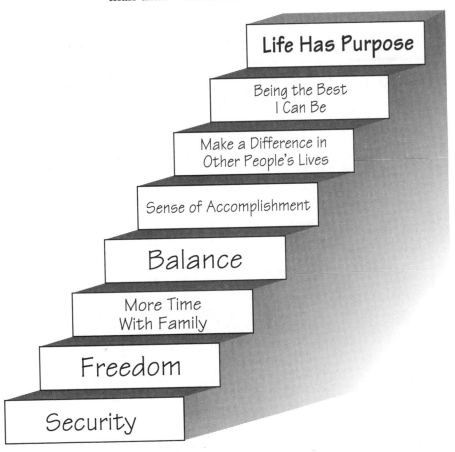

Life Has Purpose

Being the Best
I Can Be

Make a Difference in
Other People's Lives

Sense of Accomplishment

Balance

More Time
With Family

Freedom

Security

It's at the highest level where the greatest connection between your values and your financial future is made—usually seven to nine answers up the Values Staircase. The most values I've seen is seventeen. Regardless of the exact number of "stairs," every complete Values Conversation goes up three "flights," or levels.

Level 1. Easy answers about the "lower self," usually about money, material goods, security, and freedom. They're about taking care of business, creating the more immediate payoffs.

Level 2. More thoughtful responses about doing for others or being with others, such as *providing for the family, making a difference, having an impact on my community,* and *social consciousness.*

The Hierarchy of Needs

Abraham Maslow (1908–1970) was a founder of humanistic psychology and one of the few academics to study healthy individuals. He concluded that "man is a wanting animal" and that as soon as one desire is satisfied, another takes its place. The highest level of need is "self-actualization"— becoming everything you can be. Following is Maslow's hierarchy of needs, from lowest to highest.

(Level 1)
1. *Biological:* air, water, food, shelter, sex, sleep
2. *Safety:* protection from elements, disease, fear

(Level 2)
3. *Love and belongingness:* union with and affinity for others
4. *Esteem:* self-esteem and esteem by others
5. *Cognitive:* knowledge, meaning, inquiry, order
6. *Aesthetic:* beauty, balance, form

(Level 3)
7. *Self-actualization:* realizing potential, "becoming everything you can be," having "peak" experiences

---

Level 3. A significant emotional transition where you're focused on the "higher self." This can be likened to Abraham Maslow's self-actualization level, where the values take on an expansive tone and are about large, internal/emotional payoffs: *fulfillment of my destiny or purpose, becoming the best human being I can, spiritual fulfillment, being one with the universe, total inner peace, nirvana, enlightenment,* and so on.

There are generally several answers at each level, and sometimes people bounce up or down a level in the course of the conversation. But ultimately everyone can reach the third level of pure emotion. At the third level, you gain a sense of the *real* purpose of your life and can reflect on the ways smart choices about money impact all of your values.

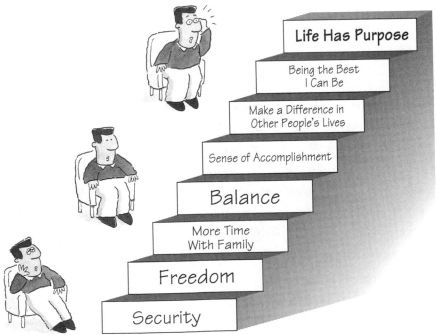

YOUR FIRST STEP: CONDUCTING THE VALUES CONVERSATION

Now you will create the vital foundation for a financial plan that is specially tailored not only to your desire for greater wealth in the future, but also to the rich *values* that are important to you today. *Values-Based Financial Planning* is about doing, not about reading nor even about learning. Before you go on to the next chapter, be sure to set aside some time to have the Values Conversation with a partner. When you meet, review the guidelines on page 18 together, then relax and enjoy. You may find it interesting to do the Values Staircase exercise with friends. It can be fun to elevate your interaction to a more meaningful level than most social chitchat. The conversation will take five to fifteen minutes, and it can spur hours of discussion afterward!

"Even though I have known 'what' to do, I never did it. The Values Conversation helped me realize that, in order to be successful, I had to learn to manage my emotions about money, finances, and investing. The process helped me clarify my values, articulate my goals, and commit to a specific strategy to meet my goals by a specific date. I found the final plan exciting and have enjoyed taking control of my future—there is no turning back!"

Daniel M. Betzel
Attorney • Pickerington, Ohio

Detailed directions for the Values Conversation appear on page 5.

continue as needed

"What's important about money *to you?*"

NAME: _____

Guidelines for an Effective Values Conversation

Choose a good partner. Work with someone who will be interested in hearing what you have to say and in supporting you in completing the exercise. Your partner has just two rules to follow: 1) Stick with the format of "What's important about ——————— *to you?*" and 2) never offer suggestions. The second one may be tough for spouses, but to help curb the urge to answer for one another, complete a separate staircase for each person. An additional blank staircase for your spouse or partner is on the opposite page.

Don't chat about your answers. Stay focused, and keep working your way up the staircase. You can discuss the answers later.

Respond thoughtfully. Usually, the first answer that comes to mind is what's true for you, but if nothing is forthcoming, be patient. It's not like a quiz show with a time limit and a buzzer if you don't answer fast enough, so take your time. At any point on the staircase, if no answer comes to you immediately, take your time. Your partner should remain silent while you are thinking.

COACHING FOR YOUR PARTNER

- Relax.
- Listen.
- Don't make suggestions.
- Don't be pushy.
- Don't interrogate.

Follow the format. Have your partner start with "What's important about money *to you?*" then follow up by substituting the last value given: "What's important about ——————— *to you?*"

Detailed directions for the Values Conversation appear on page 5.

continue as needed

"What's important about money *to you?*"

NAME: _____

Go all the way. A common mistake for people who've never really talked about their values before, much less identified them with precision, is not going far enough up the Values Staircase. Yet your most meaningful values will be revealed at the top.

The farther you go, the better you understand your financial motivations, and the more powerfully you are inspired to follow through with the rest of the steps necessary to create and implement a Values-Based Financial Plan.

Hint: If you get "stuck" at a certain level or on a particular value, put yourself in the position of having achieved that value, and ask what would be important to you about it. In the example on page 10, Terry struggled with what was important about having more time with family and creating a sense of balance. So the question became, "Once I already have created it, what's important about having balance to me?" As another example, suppose you couldn't think of anything beyond "not being a burden to others." Then you would ask yourself, "Once I know I will not be a burden to others, what's important about not being a burden to me?"

Everyone has Level-3 values, and most of us have two or three. If you find it difficult to get to Level 3, you may want to revisit the exercise later, setting aside the staircase and picking up where you left

The Question Is Not . . .

"What does money mean to you?"

"Why is money important?"

"What is it about money that's important?"

"What do you want to do with your money?"

Stick to the question exactly as it's written: *What's important about money to you?* To discover what is truly important, you must use the proper sentence structure. Trust my experience on this. The advisors I coach and their clients have done this process thousands of times, and when a variation is introduced, the results are compromised.

off another time. Continue until you can't put what you're thinking and feeling into words, until the intangible emotions are so pure that words seem inadequate.

You can miss the power of the Values Conversation if you cut it short, going only two or three steps up the Values Staircase. It's equally important that you don't try to leapfrog to the top by trying to just "figure out" what your highest financial value is. Forget it! That's too much work and it won't be your real answer anyway. You'll find the significance of this process in the crescendo of values, in seeing how each value relates to the one before it.

Once you have concluded your Values Conversation, you are ready to begin looking at your goals. But be sure to finish this vital first step before going on to the next chapter. It will clarify the goal-setting process and make it easier to complete.

CHAPTER 2

Make Meaningful Milestones: Setting Specific Goals

*He who is fixed to a star
does not change his mind.*

Leonardo da Vinci
Notebooks (c. 1500)

As a teenager, Jim and his family lived in a subsidized apartment after his father lost his accounting job. Then the whole clan worked as janitors and security personnel to help pay the rent. Jim later dropped out of high school, and they eventually lost even that small apartment and lived in a camper van. It was in the midst of this adversity that he began working as a stand-up comedian.

He bombed at first, but soon he was doing uncanny, rubber-faced impersonations of Hollywood legends. Critics praised him as the best they'd ever seen, and audiences gave him standing ovations every night. In no time, he skyrocketed to the top of his field and was earning enough to provide for his entire family before he was old enough to vote.

Do you recognize the comedian in this story? Jim Carrey's multimillion-dollar career is a modern Horatio Alger adventure. But if this were a work of fiction instead of real life, that would be the end of it. The truth is that Jim decided to completely reinvent himself. He took his bow before a standing, clapping, cheering audience—and vowed to completely change his act.

Why would he do such a thing? Why walk away from a routine that got him standing ovations every night? Jim realized his career was on the wrong path. That road would have led to headlining in Las Vegas—that's where great impressionists end up. But he had another destination in mind: He wanted to be a great comedic actor like Bob Hope, Jerry Lewis, and Dick Van Dyke. To spur himself on and to demonstrate his commitment, he wrote himself a $10 million check and put it in his billfold to hold until the day he could cash it.

Jim started introducing oddball comedic commentary and strange characters to his act, and he often flopped. His comedian peers thought he'd truly lost his mind. It must have been hard to start over, but just look where it ultimately led him. The results were some of the memorable characters he brought to the TV show *In Living Color* and the characterizations he made famous in films like *Ace Ventura: Pet Detective, The Mask,* and *Batman Forever.* Most of us have never seen him do the impersonations that generated so much acclaim, although Jim Carrey became a Hollywood phenomenon. Whether you like his work or not, you have to respect the fact that the man earns over $10 million dollars per picture (I don't suppose he's had any trouble cashing that check!) and has the luxury of pursuing only the roles that most interest him.

Chances are that you are not destitute and seeking superstardom. Nor, for that matter, that you are stand-up comic looking to revamp your career. But the lessons are valid. Few hardships are permanent. Sometimes you have to change direction even when you're succeeding. Know where you're going and why, and you *can* get there.

You've probably read statistics about people who write down their goals versus those who don't. Not surprisingly, the goalsetters outpace the others by a wide margin. Indeed, if Jim Carrey hadn't known what he wanted, he never would have achieved it.

This chapter will not spend much more time extolling the virtues of goal setting. I'm going to assume that if you're interested in planning for your financial future, you've already figured that one out. My purpose will be to get you intensely focused so you can precisely define the goals you want your money to help you achieve: What do you want, by when, exactly, and how much money will it take?

GETTING WHAT YOU REALLY WANT

Values are the intangible reasons (emotional payoffs) to create and follow a financial plan; goals are the tangible results. The first step in setting goals is a quick brainstorming session, which is more fun to do with a partner, but you can certainly do it by yourself if you prefer.

Be sure to complete this exercise before moving on to the next chapters. You'll need your notes to create the Financial Road Map in chapter 4. Have your partner ask you, "What are your tangible goals that require money and planning to achieve?" Your partner can record the ideas you generate during this brainstorm on the next page. If you get stumped, review your values from the exercise in the previous chapter: Do they lead you to want to attain a certain financial standing so you can more easily fulfill them?

What goals/tangible things or events do you want to achieve to help you experience your values? Are there milestones in your life by which you measure your success that have a financial component? Do you want to . . .

- *be financially independent?*
- *retire?*
- *send children or grandchildren to college?*
- *send yourself to college?*
- *buy a second home?*
- *take a special trip?*
- *fund a scholarship at your alma mater or establish a charity?*
- *commission a building for a hospital or your place of worship?*
- *take a year off to live in another country?*
- *create a travel fund so your kids or friends can see the world with you?*

Reach for the moon . . .Shoot for the stars!

What Are My Tangible Goals
That Require Money and Planning
to Achieve?

*Whether you are planning
the next five years
or the next fifty,
you can be on-purpose.*

Dreaming with a Deadline

No doubt you have some great ideas about how to use your money to create comfort or adventure or accomplishment for yourself and others in the future. This is a good start. Now, to really bring the goals to life, you need to set specific dates for achievement. If you want to retire, for example, you need to ask yourself, *When, exactly, do I want to be able to stop working?* You don't actually have to, but by when would you like to be able to stop working?

Choose dates that mean something to *you.*

You could decide that you wanted to stop working when you reached age sixty-five, so you can easily determine *exactly when,* including the day. You're looking for a specific answer, such as "December 12, 2020."

It's interesting that even someone who hasn't thought about this before often has no trouble coming up with a precise answer. As they think about this question, most people have the same reaction: They quickly come up with a significant date, such as a birthday, anniversary, or the first of the year.

Don't Worry About the How for Now

You may find yourself wondering if your goals are realistic. This is a legitimate concern; however, the time for realism will come after you've assessed your current financial situation, determined how much money you can invest to increase your wealth, and decided what degree of risk will be comfortable for you in achieving your goals. After this detailed analysis, you may very well find that some of your goals aren't realistic and you need to get creative, either in dreaming new dreams, generating more income, or spending less—but now is not the time to worry about that. Right now, we're laying groundwork. This should be fun!

You do need to prioritize your goals and think about what each of them will cost you. If you are working with a spouse or partner, collaborate and compromise until you agree. This can be the source of heated discussion, so just be prepared to keep a cool head. For example, one person may think paying all of a child's college expenses is more important than handling retirement needs. There is no one "right" answer for this dilemma. What if the child's college expenses are paid, but then the child has the financial burden of taking care of elderly parents? Or what if, in your family, taking care of parents in their old age is not considered a burden but a privilege? When confronting such differences, your Values Staircases can be a good guide. More often than not, the decisions you make will not be clear-cut, but you can ensure that they are based on *your* values. The idea is to plan well enough that you can take care of everything—so that priorities become somewhat irrelevant—but it's better to clarify those priorities now than later.

The future will come whether you plan for it or not. Will you have the future you want or the future that happens to you by default?

Once you've prioritized your goals, it's time to figure out how much money they will require. How much money per year will it take to have the kind of life you want after you've chosen to stop working? How much money will college cost? How much money will your vacation home cost? And so on.

Answering the questions for your own goals may require some research, such as making phone calls, checking the Internet for cost comparisons, or other similar activities. However, do *not* think about inflation or other financial factors yet; that will come later when you create your plan. Skip the complicated calculations for now and just start to figure the estimated costs per year and write them on the worksheet on pages 33–34. Here are some examples.

Sample

Goal Worksheet

Goal description: Financial Independence
Target date: April 1, 2015
Amount needed: $6,000/month
Two or three words describing the feelings and thoughts I will have when this is achieved:
Relief! Proud, relaxed, having fun.

Goal Description: Live in the south of France for six months
Target date: February 6, in 2005 (Rose's birthday)
Amount needed: $30,000
Two or three words describing the feelings and thoughts I will have when this is achieved:
Excited, curious, adventurous, free.

Goal description: Endow a scholarship fund
for young entrepreneurs

Target date: September 5, 2010

Amount needed: $10,000/year

Two or three words describing the feelings and thoughts I will have when this is achieved:
Great! Purposeful: I'm really making a
contribution to something I believe in.

Goal description: Buy a second home in Montana
and furnish it

Target date: January 1, 2001

Amount needed: $200,000 purchase price ($1,600/month
mortgage, $40,000 down payment, $20,000 furnishings)

Two or three words describing the feelings and thoughts I will have when this is achieved:
Awesome! Nurtured, expansive, in touch with
nature. I have a retreat, access to the best fly
fishing around, and a great place to bring
friends and family.

Goal description: Send Gene to college

Target date: August 1, 2010

Amount needed: $80,000

Two or three words describing the feelings and thoughts I will have when this is achieved:
Proud and responsible, generous, happy for our son.

Can you see how these goals relate directly to a person's values? Can you see, also, how much more depth they have with the values in mind? When you define your goals specifically in terms of date and cost, then give the "why" behind them, they become significantly more meaningful and motivational.

Once you've done worksheets for your own goals, you're on your way. The next step will be to assess your current financial picture so you can tell what needs to happen between now and the future to make these goals a reality. But for now, just get those goals on paper. Remember, don't worry about the "how" yet. Let's just get the "what," "when," "how much," and "why" handled first. Your values should motivate you to do the work.

Goal Worksheet

Goal description: _____

Target date: _____

Amount needed: _____

Two or three words describing the feelings and thoughts
    I will have when this is achieved:

_____

_____

_____

Goal description: _____

Target date: _____

Amount needed: _____

Two or three words describing the feelings and thoughts
    I will have when this is achieved:

_____

_____

_____

Goal description: _____

Target date: _____

Amount needed: _____

Two or three words describing the feelings and thoughts
    I will have when this is achieved:

_____

_____

_____

Goal description: _____

Target date: _____

Amount needed: _____

Two or three words describing the feelings and thoughts
    I will have when this is achieved:

_____

_____

_____

Goal description: _____

Target date: _____

Amount needed: _____

Two or three words describing the feelings and thoughts
    I will have when this is achieved:

_____

_____

_____

CHAPTER 3

BENCHMARK YOUR CURRENT FINANCIAL REALITY: GATHERING YOUR DOCUMENTS

He who knows others is learned.
He who knows himself is wise.

LAOTSE

The Character of Tao (Sixth Century B.C.)

Now that you've expanded your thinking into the realm of possibility—your dreams and goals for your financial future—it's time to return to the present. To get somewhere tomorrow, you have to know your position today. It's as if you're buying an airline ticket: To reach your destination, you have to know more than where you want to go. You also need to know where you are.

The tasks you'll complete in this chapter will help you fully grasp your current financial reality. You'll be gathering all relevant information about your assets and liabilities into one place, then either turning them over to someone else to be organized or doing it yourself. We'll further explore whether you'll want to engage a professional for this and ongoing services in later chapters. For now, we'll complete a basic checklist so you can get your bearings before takeoff.

FINANCIAL DOCUMENTS CHECKLIST

If you are one of the few individuals who can quickly and easily put your hands on all of your financial information, consider yourself well-organized. But if you can't, now's a good time to get this in order. It will be worth it, I promise. Start by simply gathering each document and putting a copy of the relevant pages in a binder or accordion file.

You're looking for statements that include the *current value* of each item. For example, to establish your income, you need the page of your federal income tax return that shows your net income, not necessarily the whole document. If you're working with a spouse or partner and you've filed separate tax returns, be sure you pull both.

Some of the items don't have a monetary value, but they are included because of their importance to your overall financial picture. For instance, although some insurance policies (such as variable life or whole life) carry a cash value, others (such as term life and automobile) don't. For those with no cash value, simply pull a statement that gives you a summary of the policy.

Financial Documents Checklist

Subject	Source
❏ **Income**	Last year's tax return
❏ **Retirement**	Most recent plan statements, such as for a company plan, 401(k), Keogh, Simplified Employee Pension (SEP), Individual Retirement Account (IRA), Registered Retirement Savings Plan (RRSP), Tax Sheltered Annuity (TSA), or other annuities
❏ **Savings**	Most recent statements from bank accounts, money market funds, certificates of deposit
❏ **Brokerage Accounts and Stock Options**	Most recent statements detailing stocks (including both stocks you've purchased and options you have not yet exercised), bonds, and mutual funds

continued on next page

Subject	Source
❏ **Insurance**	Policies or contracts for life, disability, health, auto, home owners, renters, liability, long-term care, or any other insurance
❏ **Real Estate**	Appraisals, loan information, or statements for your primary residence, as well as vacation and investment properties
❏ **Collectibles**	Appraisals of current market value for precious metals, art, and other collectibles
❏ **Business Ownership**	Current plus previous four years' balance sheets and profit-and-loss statements, as well as buyout agreements and a business valuation/appraisal if you have one (include value of stock if publicly traded)
❏ **Inheritance**	A copy of the trust, will, or other document detailing your inheritance (if available; if not, and the inheritance is certain, write the number on a piece of paper and include it)
❏ **Estate Plan**	A copy of your own will, trust, or other document detailing what you wish to be done with your assets and liabilities when you die

Now comes a critical next step, one that will require some simple addition and a little patience.* You'll be completing your own Four Quadrants™ diagram, similar to the example on the next page. If you can't find the information you need from the financial documents you've collected, consult the person who sold you the financial product. He or she should be able to walk you through the statement and help you find the bottom line.

* Of course, if you are getting queasy or restless about doing *any* math but are still committed to seeing this process through, this is your cue to call in the troops. You can set your binder or file aside and turn to chapters 6 and 7 to educate yourself about hiring a competent professional. A capable advisor can help you get organized.

Where I Am Today

Your purpose in gathering your documents is to help you ascertain whether you

1. have enough money set aside for an emergency;

2. are accumulating enough wealth to achieve your goals or to maintain your quality of life/standard of living if you have already retired;

3. have amassed too much debt, which is counter to your goals; and

4. have enough insurance to protect your plan.

The Four Quadrants diagram you'll be using to consolidate this information is part of the Financial Road Map you'll create in the next chapter. Your ultimate financial objective is to accumulate and protect as much as possible in the upper right quadrant ("Growth"); your immediate objective, however, is to see how well you've been doing so far.

Think of the Four Quadrants as a "big picture" tool.

You'll notice that each of the four quadrants (as printed on the front of the Financial Road Map) has a further division: "Now," "Want to Be," and "Action." The "Now" box conveys your current financial state. The "Want to Be" box will be filled in, either on your own or with an advisor, by applying certain financial principles, guidelines, calculations, and variables for unique situations to reflect the monetary requirements of the goals you've set. The bridge between the "Now" and the "Want to Be" box is the financial strategy ("Action"). This, too, will require extensive research or the advice of a

The Four Quadrants Worksheet

Sample

Where I Am Today　　ASSET PROFILE

CASH RESERVES		GROWTH	
Now:		Now:	
		GE Stock	$36,500
ABC Bank Savings Acct.	$5,000	Coca Cola Stock	11,000
XYZ Money Market Fund	6,000	Cash Value Variable	
Cash in safe deposit box	1,000	Universal Life Policy	156,000
		Cash Value Whole Life	17,000
	$12,000	XYZ Annuity	187,000
		IRA #1	58,000
(2 month's reserves		IRA #2	40,000
if no other income)		SEP	110,000
		ABC Bank CD	30,000
		XYZ Mutual Fund	287,000
		401 (k)	140,000
		Cash Value of	
		Company Pension	280,000
		Rental Property Equity	56,000
			$1,408,500

DEBT		RISK MANAGEMENT	
Now:			
		(Use the	
Visa	$16,000	Risk	
MasterCard	4,000	Management	
Department Store Card	1,600	Insurance	
Car Loan	27,000	Worksheet	
Mortgage	183,000	at right.)	
	$231,600	*(Note: A sample	
		Risk Management	
		worksheet is provided	
		on page 46.)*	

Your Four Quadrants Worksheet

Where I Am Today	ASSET PROFILE
CASH RESERVES	**GROWTH**
Now:	Now:

DEBT	**RISK MANAGEMENT**
Now:	(Use the Risk Management Insurance Worksheet at right.)
	(A blank Risk Management worksheet form is provided on page 47.)

(Note: This is a reduced-size version of the same worksheet printed on the back side of the Financial Road Map, which has been inserted into the back of this book.)

professional. In this chapter, we're going to concentrate only on the "Now"—the factual, current reality, the benchmark of your financial truth—and leave the others blank, since filling in those pieces will require further research if you're going to complete the Financial Road Map on your own, or an advisor's help if you're going that route. Later, you will create a financial plan to actualize the Financial Road Map. (The Financial Road Map is not the plan.)

Cash Reserves

What is the amount of cash I have on reserve right now? This is the amount of money you have *specifically earmarked* for expenses only in case of serious emergency, such as disability or the loss of a job. Don't include all of your cash simply because it's a liquid asset. If you can spend it on a down payment, vacation, car, boat, horse, surfboard, fishing gear, golf clubs, holiday gifts, etc., *it's not a cash reserve;* it's spending money. Your true cash reserves are strictly for emergencies: insurance deductibles, expenses between jobs, replacing a leaky roof, or bailing a friend out of jail. Write your answer in the "Now" box of the "Cash Reserves" quadrant, and make a note of how many months your reserves would keep you afloat if you had no other income.

Debt

How much debt do I have? Include consumer debt, as well as any loans or other liabilities. Write your answer in the "Now" box of the "Debt" quadrant.

Growth

What is the current value of my assets designated to fund my future goals? In the "Now" box of the "Growth" quadrant, include the cash value of insurance, mutual funds, stocks, bonds, stock options, or any

Debt vs. Growth

Debt is bad stuff. It's the enemy of growth. Consumer debt may have an elimination time frame of eighteen months or more. Your mortgage may just get paid off over the thirty-year term. These durations may be okay for you. Then again, they may just suck the life out of your financial future. When debt is out of proportion to your assets, it can debilitate you financially. *If debt is an issue for you, a <u>real</u> financial planner can help you, or you may want to consider a credit counselor.* In addition, you can find numerous resources on debt elimination at libraries, bookstores, and on the Internet.

Growth is the good stuff! This is the money you've invested that pays for the important things in life: college, vacation homes, financial independence, etc. It is the money you may be living off of now or will be someday. It is what you get to pass on to the people or charities you care about after you are gone to make your mark on the world.

other vehicles you're employing to increase your wealth, together with retirement plans and expected inheritance. (You may choose to exclude expected inheritances, since you can't know with certainty that your benefactors will predecease you or won't change their minds. With medical advances, choices about health and fitness, and other factors, longevity continues to increase. I encourage you to err on the conservative side, because it's better to end up with more money than not enough.)

If you don't have any assets earmarked for the future, write "None."

What is the value of my investment property? Enter the appraised value of those items you own because of their contribution to your total net worth—including vacation home(s), collectibles, precious metals, art, etc.—and that you would be willing to liquidate (sell) to fund a goal like retirement or college. If you are not going to sell your home to fund your goals, then it's not an upper-right-hand quadrant asset. Neither are your cars, furniture, or anything else you are not going to sell to raise capital to pay for your goals or provide cash flow you can spend to pay for your goals.

What is my business worth? Enter the amount from a recent appraisal or business valuation. (Be careful about overestimating the value of your business. It's not worth what *you* think it's worth; it's worth only what someone else will actually pay you for it.) For help, refer to the Society of Appraisers (www.appraisers.org). Again, your business should not go into this category if you are unwilling to sell it to fund your goals.

Risk Management

What risk management tools do I have in place? List your insurance policies' benefits by person. Include lump sum death benefits for life insurance, disability payouts for injury or illness, coverage amounts for home owners, renters, long-term care, liability, or any other policy.

Notes

What is my annual income? Use the amount from last year's tax return. You are attempting to calculate your *net spendable income.*

_____

What are my primary residence, car(s), and other "non-investment" assets worth? Enter the appraised value of those items you don't expect to liquidate for cash (sell).

_____

Now you have a basic set of financial "coordinates," your current reality: 1) your values, 2) your goals, and 3) the financial foundation on which you can build your future. You may still have unanswered questions. That's okay. So you don't have all the answers. Right now, it's more important to know the questions.

Sample

RISK MANAGEMENT•INSURANCE WORKSHEET

Use the space below to list the value of every type of insurance policy owned.

Phil
Spouse/Partner Name:

Rosemary
Spouse/Partner Name:

Policy & Value Now	Type of Policy	Policy & Value Now
$500,000 variable universal life	**Life Insurance Death Benefits** Term Life, Whole Life, Universal Life, Variable Life, etc.	$100,000 whole life
$60,000 term		$40,000 term
$560,000	*Total of All Death Benefits*	$140,000
none	**Disability**	$3K/month
HMO, 80% coverage	**Health**	PPO, 90% coverage
$500,000	**Homeowner's/Renter's**	(same)
Lexus: injury, prop. damage, med., comp., collis., $250 ded.	**Auto**	Jeep: injury, prop. damage, med., comp., collis., $250 ded.
none	**Long-Term Care**	none
none	**Critical Illness**	none
none	**Liability**	none
none	**Other**	none

RISK MANAGEMENT•INSURANCE WORKSHEET

Use the space below to list the value of every type of insurance policy owned.

Spouse/Partner Name: _____

Spouse/Partner Name: _____

Policy & Value Now	Type of Policy	Policy & Value Now
	Life Insurance **Death Benefits** Term Life, Whole Life, Universal Life, Variable Life, etc.	
	Total of All Death Benefits	
	Disability	
	Health	
	Homeowner's/Renter's	
	Auto	
	Long-Term Care	
	Critical Illness	
	Liability	
	Other	

(Note: This is a reduced-size variation of the same worksheet printed on the back side of the Financial Road Map, which has been inserted into the back of this book.)

Assessing and Managing Risk

R isk management refers to what you've done to mitigate any financial emergencies. Simply put, you either get insurance or accept the risk. Insurance can be a bit of a mind bender because it's something we purchase hoping we never need it. The key here is to make your decisions on purpose. Set aside any squeamishness you have about thinking about "the worst" (death, disability, and the like), and focus on how you can make these things work for you and your family. Know what the risk is, and know what it will cost to transfer that risk to someone (a company) with deeper pockets than you.

You may have heard the adage, "You don't know what you don't know." Now, at least, you're becoming aware of what you don't know about financial planning. At the same time, you have everything you need to either proceed with a financial professional or roll up your sleeves and get to work building your own plan.

But before we jump into a deep discussion about whether "to be advised, or not to be advised," you can create a powerful visual encapsulation of what you've done so far, which will aid you in your financial journey regardless of the road you take.

CHAPTER 4

INSPIRE YOURSELF TO ACTION: CREATING THE FINANCIAL ROAD MAP

To have his path made clear for him is the aspiration of every human being in our beclouded and tempestuous existence.

JOSEPH CONRAD
The Mirror of the Sea (1906)

Top financial professionals do a number of things financial product salespeople don't. Among them are caring about such important issues as their clients' values and helping them grasp the "big picture." To help them do this, a tool I've developed and teach to some of the best advisors in the business is the Financial Road Map, which you can create for yourself right now.

Sample

Financial Road Map®
for Living Life on Purpose

*"There are those who travel and
those who are going somewhere.
They are different, and yet they are the same.
Successful people have this over their rivals:
they know where they are going."*
Mark Caine

Where I Am Today

CASH RESERVES		GROWTH	
Now	Want to Be	Now	Want to Be
$12,000 (2 months)		$1,408,500	
Action:		Action:	

DEBT		RISK MANAGEMENT	
Now	Want to Be	Now	Want to Be
$231,600		See Insurance Worksheet on back side of Road Map	
Action:		Action:	

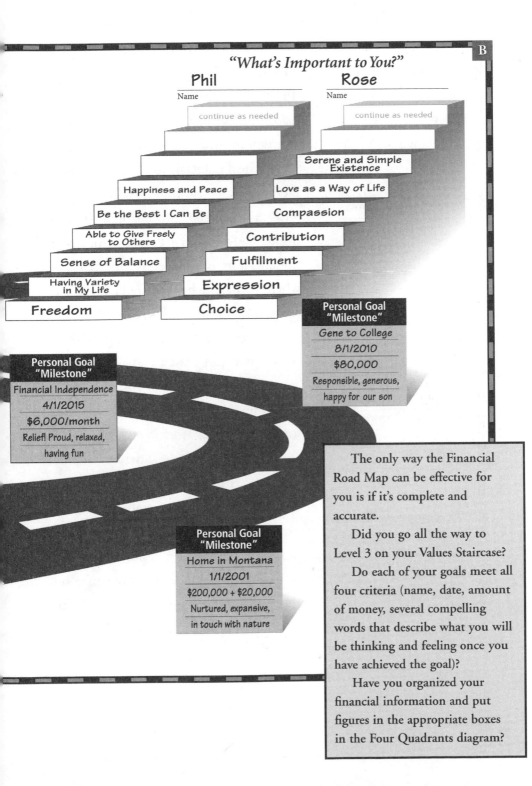

B

"What's Important to You?"

Phil
Name

Rose
Name

Phil's staircase:
- continue as needed
- Happiness and Peace
- Be the Best I Can Be
- Able to Give Freely to Others
- Sense of Balance
- Having Variety in My Life
- Freedom

Rose's staircase:
- continue as needed
- Serene and Simple Existence
- Love as a Way of Life
- Compassion
- Contribution
- Fulfillment
- Expression
- Choice

Personal Goal "Milestone"
Gene to College
8/1/2010
$80,000
Responsible, generous, happy for our son

Personal Goal "Milestone"
Financial Independence
4/1/2015
$6,000/month
Relief! Proud, relaxed, having fun

Personal Goal "Milestone"
Home in Montana
1/1/2001
$200,000 + $20,000
Nurtured, expansive, in touch with nature

The only way the Financial Road Map can be effective for you is if it's complete and accurate.

Did you go all the way to Level 3 on your Values Staircase?

Do each of your goals meet all four criteria (name, date, amount of money, several compelling words that describe what you will be thinking and feeling once you have achieved the goal)?

Have you organized your financial information and put figures in the appropriate boxes in the Four Quadrants diagram?

The purpose of the Financial Road Map is not only to give you perspective, but it is also designed to keep you inspired to follow through on pursuing the quality of life you desire for yourself and those you love. Incorporating the results of each of the processes we've done so far, your Financial Road Map should engage you and make real the financial future you have determined you want.

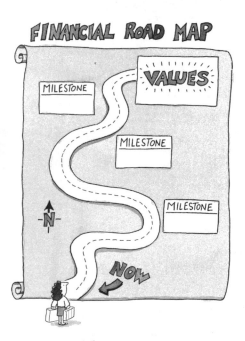

The essence of the Financial Road Map is to demonstrate how you will bridge the gap between where you are now and where you want to be so you can enjoy the tangible payoff of reaching your goals and the emotional payoff of experiencing your values.

The Financial Road Map can also facilitate a meaningful conversation with a financial professional if you decide you'd like to get some help. Upon presentation of this clear summary of where you are, where you're headed, and what makes you tick, you'll know immediately if you're dealing with a person you can trust to advise you in a comprehensive plan or if you're meeting someone who just wants to sell you some insurance, stocks, or some other "hot" product. If the advisor takes a genuine interest in what you've prepared, appreciates your thorough examination of your own motives and needs, and expresses a desire to help you achieve your goals, you know you're on the right track. Then you can talk in detail about each aspect of the Financial

Road Map and share the information in your financial binder or file, and the advisor will be able to give you an excellent sense of your next steps.

If you're planning to go it alone, there's nothing like a visual reminder of why you're putting in all the effort to make this plan happen. You'll want to review your Financial Road Map at least once a month to help you focus on the reasons for your hard work. This way, you can feel rewarded as you go along, not just when you achieve a specific goal: You'll know the time you spend has a meaningful purpose and will ultimately lead to the results that are most important *to you.*

So let's get started. There are no more calculations to do for now. This project should be fun and quick to finish. Your own 17" x 22" full-color blank Financial Road Map was placed inside the back cover of this book at the time of binding. If you find it's missing—or, to order additional copies of the map—please call Bachrach & Associates, Inc. at (800) 347-3707.

"The Financial Road Map concept is ideal for the serious investor. Being able to compare our holdings with our needs has led my wife, Ruth, and me to a financial plan that gives us peace of mind and maximum control of our funds. Our Financial Road Map is a terrific tool for managing our future."

Jerry L. Mercer
Retired Professor • Lexington, Kentucky

WHERE I AM TODAY

Let's focus first on the box in the lower left corner, "Where I Am Today." Simply transfer the information from your Four Quadrants on page 41 to the smaller version on your Financial Road Map. You will have to abbreviate, but make it as complete as possible. You'll notice each of the quadrants has a "Now" box and one for "Want to Be," or the future, as well as one for "Action." You can use these boxes later when you either create a financial plan for yourself or work with someone else to do it for you.

PERSONAL GOALS/"MILESTONES"

Shift your attention to the milestone boxes along the road. Here you can record the goals you set forth in chapter 2. Refer to pages 33–34, and in the first personal goal box write down a phrase that captures the essence of your first goal, such as "Move to bigger home (2,500 sq. ft.)." Note the date you are planning to achieve this goal and the amount of money you've determined you need to do it. Also include two or three words that describe what you will be thinking and feeling once this goal is achieved.

Do the same for each of the goals you listed. If you have more than three, feel free to draw and fill in boxes of your own.

You Can Have It All

Seeing your goals nestled in your current financial picture may make you wonder whether they can be realized or not. This is the Big Question for financial planners: whether and how the available assets can meet the future goals. To arrive at a legitimate answer requires a level of knowledge addressed in the next chapter, but I can give you a hint if you are one of the inspired few who prefer to make their income match their goals rather than fit their goals within their income.

I'm a big believer in having it all, at least anything you want. I also believe you should decide how much is enough for you. If you have control over your income (and I believe everyone can), you can craft an *income strategy* to realize a fabulous lifestyle today and establish a secure and fantastic financial independence for the future.

To do this, you have to be willing to earn a lot more money than you actually need today.

1. Decide how much spendable income you need for your lifestyle. How much do you need to really enjoy yourself today? Let's say the amount is $200,000 a year.

2. Figure out the amount of assets you need to generate the income your lifestyle requires. A five percent after-tax return is conservative and realistic, so take your lifestyle figure and divide by five percent ($200,000 ÷ .05 = $4,000,000). You can choose some other percentage, but be careful not to be greedy or unrealistic. Realism is more important than

continued on next page

optimism in this case: it's better to end up with more rather than less money than you need. I realize many people have been fortunate to earn a fifteen percent or higher return on their money; however, you can't count on this over a period of ten or more years—in fact, you can't count on it at all. A five percent *after-tax* return is a good deal.

3. Do the math. Figure out how much money you need to save to have your assets pay for your lifestyle without you working. First establish a date (for our example let's use 12/31/09 and pretend it's 1/1/00 today) and an estimated rate of return on your investments (eight percent is conservative and realistic). Now consult an online future value calculator or use the chart that follows for a rough estimate. If you were to go to financial planning school, you'd discover this calculation is not perfect—such factors as state income tax, deductible contributions to retirement accounts, and other factors tend to skew the numbers—but this gives you a reasonable target for your income.

4. Recalculate your income goals. Alas, that doesn't mean that $300,000 a year will do it; Uncle Sam wants his share, and you have living expenses in the meanwhile. The question now becomes, "How much gross income do I need to earn each year to do three things: Save/invest for financial independence, pay my taxes, and pay for my current lifestyle?"

Future Value Calculations
Based on an Eight Percent Return Over Ten Years, Investing Once a Month

Payment Amount	Future Balance
$100	$18,294.60
$500	$91,473.01
$1,000	$182,946.03
$5,000	$914,730.17
$10,000	$1,829,460.35
$15,000	$2,744,190.52
$20,000	$3,658,920.70
$25,000	$4,573,650.87
$30,000	$5,488,381.05

If you want to spend $200,000 per year on your current lifestyle *and* save/invest enough to have a $200,000 annual income without working ($4 million), you need to earn a gross income of about:

$200,000	current lifestyle
$300,000	annual savings
$350,000	taxes (maybe more with state tax)
$850,000	**gross annual income**

Again, this is not a perfect number, but you get the idea. Some people like to know what to do with what they've got. Others want to know what they have to do to get what they want.

WHAT'S IMPORTANT

You'll finish the Financial Road Map by returning to your ultimate purpose: fulfilling your values. There are two Values Staircases so you and a spouse or partner can use one Financial Road Map, assuming you pool your wealth and share the same financial goals.

Refer to the values hierarchy you worked on in chapter 1. As you rewrite your values on the Financial Road Map, enjoy reexperiencing the emotions you felt when you were first constructing your Values Staircase. How does each value make you feel? When you see each value leading to the next, do you sense their connection and power in your life?

Once you have written all of your values on the Financial Road Map, stand back and allow their impact on your goals and current financial reality, and vice versa, to really hit home. Allow the gap represented on this map—the distance between now and the future, as well as the remaining unanswered questions—to become a catalyst for you in moving forward and doing whatever it takes to achieve your goals and fulfill your values. You deserve nothing less.

"As a former elementary school principal, I wanted my financial planning to be organized and follow something like the weekly lesson plans I had completed when I was a teacher and that I required of my teachers when I was a principal. With my husband owning a deadline-oriented graphics business, he had no time for orchestrating a financial plan, and we were wallowing in a sea of financial disorganization. After interviewing thirteen financial planners, one offered us the Financial Road Map, which presented an organized, clear-cut method that would target our needs for years to come. After our interview, we reviewed our path to our future with our new advisor so we could revise and stay the course for what is down the road.

The map metaphor helped us become aware of where we are now, how diversified we can be, how many forks in the road we can afford to take, and what happens when we reach our retirement destination. Our advisor developed a clear, concise financial plan, which is our guide to the future. Without it, we would not be financially solvent and totally aware of where we are going."

Carole Farmer
Retired Elementary School Principal • Overland Park, Kansas

"HOW CAN I GET THE MOST FOR MY MONEY?"

Now that you've gathered all the information needed to begin building a plan, it's time to decide whether or not you want to proceed alone or get professional help. If you haven't completed the checklist for section 1, go back and do the exercises you've neglected now. You'll need to have them done to make a wise decision about what comes next.

SECTION 2 CHECKLIST

✔ Date Completed

❑ _____ Decide whether you're a Do-it-yourselfer, Collaborator, or Delegator.

❑ _____ Interview potential advisors.

❑ _____ Complete the Trusted Advisor checklist for all advisors you interview.

❑ _____ Review the checklists for sections 1 and 2 and take *action* on anything that remains to be done.

❑ _____ Reward yourself for completing all the exercises in this book!

CHAPTER 5

KNOW YOURSELF: DECIDING WHETHER OR NOT YOU NEED HELP

No man can produce great things who is not thoroughly sincere in dealing with himself.

JAMES RUSSELL LOWELL
Rousseau and the Sentimentalists (1870)

"So, what do you do?" It's an innocent-enough question, but it turned out to be loaded with philosophical importance for one friend of mine, John Hansch.

He was dining out with his family and, since his kids were about the same age as some others at the restaurant, the youngsters started playing together. Naturally, the parents started talking, and they quickly got around to the subject of occupations.

It turned out that the fellow at the next table was a neurosurgeon. John is a financial advisor. When the neurosurgeon learned this, his eyes lit up. "Wow," he said. "That's great. The market's kind of a hobby of mine."

He was probably about the same age as John, who's in his early forties. What made the exchange so memorable for John was not only his surprise that the good doctor would spend what little discretionary time he had on learning about and playing the stock market, but also that he was obviously neglecting his health, of all things, to do it. He was seriously overweight.

Here was a fellow who no doubt understood the implications of obesity on his physical health, longevity, and, therefore, on his young family, but he was choosing to invest his time and attention in the market. He may have even justified it to himself as something he did for his family. Yet if we'd had the chance to ask why he didn't make his health a hobby—something that would more directly benefit his family in the long run—he would probably have told us that he has *no time* for exercise.

Yet if this man is like other people who make finances their hobby, he doesn't spend just a few minutes a day on it. Chances are he spends anywhere from a half-hour to two hours a day dealing with and thinking about money. He may call his broker a couple of times, he may check his stocks or mutual funds in the paper or on the Web, he may watch a financial show or two, or read some financial publications—it's easy to burn thirty minutes or more a day. With basic Internet technology, it's tempting to stay online all day long.

The obvious question is why he has the time to manage the money and no time for his health. Why not delegate what he can, and spend his time on what's important? No one else can do his exercise for him. No one else can spend time with his kids for him. But the stock market? There are plenty of people qualified and competent to invest for him. Maybe he's just lost sight of his priorities. Surely he knows his health is more important than money.

Many people mistakenly move money up the priority list because the people who sell financial products, magazines, and information spend a lot of advertising money and salespeople's time trying to convince them they should. Another friend, John Bowen, who's a principal in a major asset management firm, calls it "financial pornography" because of its superficial allure and its appeal to a base desire: greed. Much of the financial services industry pummels you with information, making you feel that if you don't know all about finance, you're stupid or at least inadequate.

But you shouldn't have to know it all—unless you want to and you really do have the time for it. So if you are going to do it yourself, at least be sure not to sacrifice what's really important in the long-run.

Chapters 3 and 4 left you with a number of unanswered questions, which meant significant blanks on your Financial Road Map. You haven't yet mastered all there is to know to fill these in yet, and, frankly, giving you that level of expertise is beyond the scope of this book. It may be beyond the scope of any nontechnical instruction. While some books offer you rules of thumb to determine such things as required cash reserves or the amount of insurance you need, we won't be taking any shortcuts here. It's important for you to understand that these sweeping guidelines are not the best way to calculate your financial needs, and especially not the best way to create a customized financial plan. A plan designed to maximize your current financial resources will require more sophisticated understandings and a more comprehensive approach.

If you are going to do your plan yourself, you will need to become at least as educated as a professional so you can give yourself financial advice based on the same body of knowledge. You wouldn't rely on an incompetent financial planner, so don't rely on yourself if you are not committed to your own competency. If you're serious about your financial future, your finances cannot be your hobby any more than you would start a family as a diversion. If you are dedicated, you can no doubt do as good a job as a professional. It may require many hours up front to educate yourself, and up to four hours a week to implement and monitor your plan, but it can be done. On the other hand, if you don't have the time, patience, or enthusiasm to learn what you must, hire someone to help you.

What It Takes to Write an Effective Financial Plan

Following is an overview of the topics you or a professional will need to have mastered to create an effective plan that actualizes your Financial Road Map. It is a much-abbreviated list based on the minimum requirements for earning a Certified Financial Planner (CFP) designation.

Proper insurance coverage/risk management. Policy analysis: types of insurance policies, provisions, and riders; yield on assets, mortality/morbidity, lapses, and expenses; factors affecting suitability; contractual provision versus illustrations; crediting methods, cost and cost-comparison methods, duration of coverage, guarantees, dividend histories, industry analysis, replacement forms, insurability, and non-contestability. Types of annuities: Immediate and deferred.

Types of insurance:

Life insurance: whole, term, universal, and variable

Disability insurance/business overhead expense

Health insurance

Long-term care insurance

Homeowners insurance

Auto insurance

Commercial insurance

Other liability insurance, such as umbrella, professional, errors and omissions, directors and officers.

Cash flow analysis and budgeting. Cash management, emergency fund planning, liquidity. Assessing financial status, including assets, liabilities, cash flow, debt management; capital needs, as well as special circumstances such as divorce or remarriage, charitable planning, disabled child needs, adult-dependent needs, education needs, terminal illness planning, and closely held business planning.

Debt management. Using and reducing debt

Asset management. Home equity, types of mortgages, buying versus leasing, refinancing.

Investment returns. Types of return: annualized, real, total, risk-adjusted, after-tax, holding period, internal rates. Yields: yield-to-maturity, yield-to-call, after-tax, and realized compound.

Bond and stock valuation methods. Capitalized earnings, dividend growth, price/earnings, intrinsic value.

continued on next page

Investment theory and strategies. Portfolio performance measurement, benchmarking portfolios, risk-adjusted returns, modern portfolio theory, time- versus dollar-weighted return, dollar-cost averaging, dividend reinvestment, "active" and "passive" strategies (market timing, securities selection, bond swaps, indexed portfolios, maturity selection, buy/hold, immunization), hedging and options, pricing models.

Tax planning considerations and computations. Ethics, fundamentals, compliance, terminology, gross income, adjusted gross income, itemized deductions, taxable income, tax liability, accounting methods, and tax characteristics of business forms.

Business knowledge. Ways of taking title, forms of business, contracts.

Estate planning. Documents, strategies, tax exposures, wills, trusts.

Projections and recommendations. Financial position; cash flow; estate tax; capital needs at retirement, death, disability, or for special needs; income tax; employee benefits; risk.

Implementing the plan. Assisting clients in implementing recommendations and coordinating as necessary with other professionals, such as accountants, attorneys, real estate agents, investment advisors, stock brokers, and insurance agents.

Monitoring the plan. Evaluating the soundness of recommendations, reviewing the progress of the plan, discussing and evaluating changes in personal circumstances, evaluating based on changes in tax laws and economic circumstances.

To see the entire detailed list of topics—along with the amount of importance and desired cognitive level the CFP Board of Standards sets for them—go to the *General Information Booklet* page online (www.cfp-board.org/cert_gibtpx.html). You'll find an abundance of information about the qualifications of CFPs, including what they need to know to become certified and what they have to continue to learn to keep that certification. At this writing, CFPs are required to complete an additional thirty hours of training in subjects that contribute to increasing their professional competency.

3 WAYS TO PLAY: BE A DO-IT-YOURSELFER, A COLLABORATOR, OR A DELEGATOR

This chapter will assist you in figuring out what's next for you: doing it yourself, having someone help but doing most of it yourself, or delegating the planning and maintenance to a professional.

Option #1

Do-it-yourselfers write their own plans, conduct their own research, make their own computations, set up their own accounts—they're like a one-man-band of finances. You are better off on your own if you simply don't want to work with someone else. Or if you enjoy managing your own money a great deal and are capable of doing so, it could make sense, though not necessarily. Of course, if you don't trust anybody to help you or you feel that you must have absolute control at all times, you'll *have* to do it yourself.

What is your best source for all the information you'll need? The ideal would be for you to train to become a CFP, and you could thereby give yourself professional-quality advice without actually hiring a professional. If you have a high enough degree of interest in doing your own financial plan, perhaps you have interest in creating plans for other people, too. If not, there are a few other options, less comprehensive but valuable nonetheless.

You can do some reading. Bookstores are crammed with how-to books on personal finance. Some attempt to simplify it, some to spiritualize it, still others to promote a specific investment strategy. There is no want for books, so you won't have any trouble finding them, but once you do, how do you know which one to read? Ask around before you go to the bookstore. Do you know someone who seems to be financially responsible and successful? Ask that person for book recommendations. Read book reviews, including those offered by book buyers online.

Of course, Web-based resources are plentiful, too. Through the Internet, you can use specialized calculators for financial formulas, subscribe to e-newsletters, input a profile of yourself and your preferences to receive tailored information, access all kinds of financial data, and even read popular financial publications.

Regardless of whether the material is printed or electronic, your criteria for a good resource are simple:

❏ *Does it help me fill in the blanks on my Financial Road Map?*

❏ *Does it teach me about the topics CFPs are required to learn?*

You can also consult an insurance agent, stockbroker, or financial planner. The obvious upside of talking to someone who sells financial products for a living is that he or she will have studied those products, or at least one company's products, in great detail. Insurance agents, for example, should have no trouble telling you what coverage is generally recommended for someone in your position. (You may not want to get on their prospect lists, however, because these people will do their jobs and follow up. And follow up. And follow up. After all, a good salesperson is persistent.)

Once you've canvassed family, friends, publications, books, the Internet, and salespeople, you'll need to sit down and sort it out for yourself. Or, if you find that it all seems rather overwhelming, you may want to go back to some of the salespeople you've consulted to help you further. This would make you a *Collaborator*.

Option #2

Collaborators want to do it themselves, but they also want a relationship with a professional so they'll have someone to lean on for information and occasionally for advice. Some want an advisor to educate them, do their research for them, and confirm their own research. The Collaborator tries to balance the control of a Do-it-yourselfer with the peace of mind of a Delegator, and uses professional support as a safety net.

This is a half-in, half-out approach. The best financial advisors tend to shy away from Collaborators, although you may get lucky. If you decide to take the collaborative approach, you may be relegated to the product salespeople who, simply by the nature of the business, will give you information and assistance merely because they believe it will ultimately help them sell you a product. There are limits to the quality and breadth of information you can get from such people, so Collaborators still have to do a lot of research on their own, or persist until they find a Trusted Advisor who's willing to collaborate.

There is a saying: Attorneys who represent themselves have fools for clients. Beware a similar trap if you plan to do your own financial planning: Collaborators and Do-it-yourselfers tend to focus so much on individual products and short-term performance that they lose sight of the big picture. As a Collaborator or Do-it-yourselfer, it will be that much more important for you to revisit your Financial Road Map and stick to your plan. You'll have to be vigilant in not letting yourself be seduced by financial pornography, swayed by friends, or led astray by your own ego.

Option #3

Delegators comprise an entirely different breed. They differentiate what they can confidently hand off to someone else from what they must take care of themselves. They are not remotely interested in doing the research and strategizing, although most could do it if they wanted to. As complex as financial planning can be, just about anyone could do it. Delegators choose not to because they believe they benefit from the value a Trusted Advisor provides: to free them from having to worry about their money so they can focus on other, more important things in life. They are do-it-yourselfers only in the realms where it counts: family, friends, career, physical health, spiritual life. Otherwise, they are happy to pay competent professionals to do the rest.

One online trading company's commercial featured a classic Do-it-yourselfer sitting on a dock in front of his yacht and reciting his mantra: "Why would I pay someone else to do what I can do for myself?" Indeed, why? The Do-it-yourselfers and Collaborators have found an ally in companies like E*trade—these discount online brokers can provide valuable information to the person who has the time and inclination to seek it out.

But the Delegator has an answer to that question: "I pay someone else to manage my money so I can do all the things I can't pay someone else to do: exercise, go to my kids' soccer games, spend quiet time at home, take vacations, grow personally, improve my professional skills, enjoy my retirement, volunteer my time to worthy causes, meditate, read great books, have dinner with friends . . ." The Delegators' mantra? "Why would I do anything myself that I could pay someone else to do?"

Delegators are not interested in working with a financial professional as a reliable information resource. They're just as capable as the next person of reading the papers and magazines, surfing the 'net, and availing themselves of the services of the library. Yet they want a Trusted Advisor, someone who will maintain a high level of expertise and can be counted on to do what's in their clients' best interests. Delegators don't regard the advisor with unwarranted awe, however. It's not "I think you're so smart that I want to know what you know." Instead, it's "I trust you so much, I'll do what you tell me to do."

A man is rich in proportion to the number of things which he can afford to let alone.

— HENRY DAVID THOREAU

It may seem easy for me to promote delegating financial matters when I have been on the inside of the financial industry and understand how it works. But here's an example from my own life where I trusted someone else (actually, a number of people) in an area far outside my expertise, and I achieved the results I desired.

On October 3, 1998, I completed the Hawaii Ironman triathlon. The 2.4-mile ocean swim, 112-mile bike ride, and 26.2-mile marathon run, held in the hot, windy conditions of the lava fields on the Big Island of Hawaii, is considered the toughest single-day athletic event in the world. You've probably seen the event on TV and witnessed some of the fittest athletes in the world reduced to lumps of crawling flesh struggling to cross the finish line. My goal was twofold: 1) finish, and 2) finish without needing medical care. I knew I would not be the thrill of victory story, and I wanted to be sure I wouldn't be the agony of defeat feature, either.

My coach was none other than six-time Hawaii Ironman champion Mark Allen. In ten months, Mark helped me transform myself from a twice-a-week runner to an Ironman finisher. I was an active person, but I had never been an athlete. I hadn't run cross-country or been on the swim team. The distances seemed a bit mind-boggling, but every time I'd watched the race on TV, I'd fantasized that someday it would be me crossing that finish line.

Mark Allen is arguably the greatest triathlete in history. He is the only champion of the Hawaii Ironman to win six times in six tries. He is the oldest champion (37), and he recorded the greatest comeback victory in the history of the event.

It would be impossible for me ever to know what Mark knows about the triathlon. Mark was a virtual lab rat for endurance athletic discoveries. He and his peers accomplished things that doctors and scientists weren't sure were possible until they did them. His failures and successes over fifteen years of being totally immersed in endurance sports at the highest level could never be transferred to me. What made Ironman possible for me was not trying to know what Mark knows, but simply doing what Mark told me to do. *Results come from doing, not from knowing.*

John Collins, the retired Navy Commander who created the Hawaii Ironman, had this printed on the first flyer for the first Ironman in 1978:

SWIM 2.4 MILES

BIKE 112 MILES

RUN 26.2 MILES

AND BRAG FOR THE REST OF YOUR LIFE!

I was able to harness Mark's experience and the experience Mark had gained from his trusted advisors to earn my bragging rights. Without needing medical care!

I could never have achieved my Ironman goal if I had not delegated other things in my life to free up the time to train. I had a business to run and a life to lead. I also could never hope to learn everything about exercise physiology and success in endurance events. I could only succeed by relying on the expertise of Mark Allen and my other coaches. My quality of life is enhanced by my Ironman experience. It was made possible by being a delegator.

So let me say this, with all due respect. You ain't never gonna get it! You are almost certainly never *really* going to understand how markets work, why one insurance policy is better than another, or how global events affect your investments. The brightest financial minds in the world debate these issues ad nauseum, people who have spent their entire lives immersing themselves in economics and being students of how events affect the financial world. It's their full-time job. And any belief that you have figured it out, or are going to figure it out, *in your spare time* may be an illusion created by your ego to humor you into thinking you are smarter than you really are. It's okay. Let it go.

My friend Doug Carter says, "'The truth will set you free' is more than a religious statement." The beauty is that you, as a Delegator, don't have to understand it to get the benefit of it. This is a wonderfully freeing discovery. Financial success is derived from the doing, not the knowing.

Even the fast-food giants understand this principle of benefitting from OPK, or "Other People's Knowledge." McDonald's, the world's largest and most successful fast-food franchise, spends millions of dollars each year on site planning and employs a score of people whose job it is to research each potential location. McDonald's uses a formula that takes into consideration many variants: size of the area, growth patterns, tax rates, traffic count, neighboring commercial success rate, etc. Out of all this compiled information they pick locations and build brand-spanking-new red and yellow structures complete with towering arches.

Burger King also has a site-planning team. Their formula for deciding where to build a restaurant is much simpler: They wait for McDonald's to announce their newest location, then go out and buy land across the street.

Which is right? They both are. Certainly no one will argue with the success of a strategy with "over billions and billions served." Though not as complex, Burger King's model works just as well and saves hundreds of thousands of dollars. The two successful companies have at least one thing in common: They both get great locations.

Likewise, I didn't have to know what Mark Allen knows about human physiology or get a Vulcan mind-meld of everything he learned from his racing experience. I just did what he told me to do. And, believe me, the experience of competing in Ironman was exhilarating and the finisher's medal feels like my own personal gold medal. And I'll never really understand how and why the human mind and body are capable of so much.

"I am a later-in-life single person. It has been very beneficial to have someone like Rod, my advisor, in my life to talk with about my goals and what's important to me. The Financial Road Map was very helpful as we discussed my goals and where I wanted and needed to go. It caused me to think more clearly about my life in terms of the future, which I hadn't thought about much before. It has caused me to be more aware and has increased my commitment to reach my goals so I can enjoy what is important to me. I highly recommend that you have a financial advisor who you can trust and who can help you understand what you need to do to reach your goals, as well as give you guidance along the way."

Carolyn Megee
Sales Manager • Overland Park, Kansas

"Both my husband and I provide cost controls on projects through resource planning, cost estimating, and cost budgeting. We felt our combined experience ensured our finances/investments were well-managed. With the assistance of our Trusted Advisor, we have discovered that diversifying our investments has increased our prospects for early retirement. Additionally, our finances/investments could excel far beyond what we had imagined! The Financial Road Map is an inspiring tool."

Brigitte Landry
Cost Budgeting and Control Specialist • Anchorage, Alaska

CHOOSE THE APPROACH THAT'S RIGHT FOR YOU

When you were reading about the Do-it-yourselfer, Collaborator, and Delegator, probably one description sounded more appealing to you. To choose the approach that's right for you, keep this question foremost in your mind: *How will my decision impact my ability to create the quality of life I desire?* Remember: That's what it's all about. It's not about your money per se. It's about managing your money in a way that allows you to fulfill your values, achieve your goals, and make your life the way you really want it to be. Perhaps the most important choice is a life choice, whether to be a Do-it-yourselfer, a Collaborator, or Delegator.

You may be asking yourself, *Will doing it myself, collaborating, or delegating make me more financially successful?* Let me answer your question with one of my own.

Here's the scenario: Person A is a Do-it-Yourselfer or a Collaborator. This person has learned everything about a particular mutual fund:

- The manager, her style, background, education, experience, track record, etc.
- The type of stocks that are invested in and how these stocks will be impacted by global events, a booming economy or recession, declining or rising interest rates, a republican government vs. a democratic one
- What legislation is pending that could affect the securities in the fund
- The amount of latitude the manager has to deviate from the stated purpose of the fund

- The tax efficiency of the fund
- How the manager selects the initial universe of securities from which she will apply her method or buy criteria until she has invested in the securities that will make up the fund
- The manager's sell criteria for the securities in the fund
- The balance of assets in the fund between stocks, bonds, and cash—and how this balance affects the total return
- The overall volatility of the underlying securities in the fund and how that impacts the total return on a risk-adjusted basis
- How many stars Morningstar gives the fund
- The top 10 holdings of the fund, who their leadership and management teams are, and their business plan for growing the company
- How a change in leadership at these firms would impact their success
- What happens to the fund if the manager changes firms and how frequently this manager jumps from one company to another

This is not a complete list of everything Person A knows about the fund, because there is so much more that the investor who claims to be educated would have to know to make a truly informed decision. But you get the picture that Person A did the homework and has a pretty good understanding of what this fund is all about.

On the same day, Person B buys the same fund as Person A, then holds it for the same period of time and sells it on the same day in the future. Unlike Person A, Person B followed the advice of a Trusted Advisor and knows absolutely nothing about the mutual fund.

Who gets the better return?

Hint: This is the McDonald's versus Burger King story all over again.

How the choice is made makes no difference to the economic outcome. The financial results are the same. But who enjoyed *a better quality of life?*

I also don't buy the claim that you earn a higher return when you work with an advisor, special methodology, etc. Although there is statistical support for having an advisor if you compare the results of a bad Do-it-yourselfer with a good advisor, the real reason for hiring a Trusted Advisor is delegation, not to get a higher return.

It's not the purpose of this book to strong-arm you into seeking the services of an advisor. On the other hand, I promised to tell it like it is, and the fact is that, given a finite number of hours in the day, many people who genuinely care about their financial well-being really *shouldn't* be choosing to spend time on it every day. In many cases, this job should be completely delegated. Remember the neurosurgeon at the beginning of this chapter? Clearly, the man is bright enough to recognize that his physical health and time with family are more important than being financially astute. Yet the more important has somehow been subordinated to the less important.

The exercise you're about to do is designed to focus you on what's most important in your life (again), and to help you further discern what activities will contribute the most to your *quality* of life. The "Quality of Life Enhancer Worksheet™" is based on two principles: 1) The more you can align your behavior with your core values (what's important to you), the happier, more satisfied, and fulfilled you'll be; and 2) the more you delegate what's less important, the more time you have for what's more important.

These principles follow two basic facts of life.

1. There are only 168 hours in a week, no matter your age, how much money you make, what you've invested, how attractive you are, or how much information you can access on the Internet. No exemptions. Your quality of life is a function of how you choose to spend that time.

"Time is the stuff life is made of."

—BENJAMIN FRANKLIN
(Quoted in Franklin Planner™ products)

---

2. Some things cannot be delegated, and some things can. Question: Is delegation a privilege reserved for the elite? Answer: Hardly! Did you or any of your friends receive an allowance for doing chores around the house? That's "parental delegation." Did you notice your dad never paid you to go fishing or to play golf for him? I learned the power of delegation from my parents, who were not wealthy or elite. Everyone can delegate to one degree or another.

The Quality of Life Enhancer is designed to help you keep financial management in perspective. In the example on the next page, you see six categories down the left side of the grid. Feel free to customize these for yourself; they're not set in stone. Yet I've chosen them because in workshops on this subject, I've discovered that people can usually agree that these six are more important than money. The rest of the grid is pretty self-explanatory.

Roy Disney once said, "When your values are clear, your decisions are easy." I'd have to add that when your values are clear and

The Quality of Life Enhancer Worksheet™

NAME: Chris

Sample

Life Quality	Delegatable? I'd Like to Spend on This	More Hours Per Week to improve this area of my life?	What are three activities I would do this week
Being Healthy	☐ Yes ☑ No	4 hrs.	• Exercise 3–4 times a week. • Learn about healthier eating. • Learn yoga, and get a massage every other week.
Being Spiritual	☐ Yes ☑ No	3 hrs.	• Seek answers to my questions about God. • Go to church. • Pray or meditate daily.
Nurturing Family Relationships	☐ Yes ☑ No	4 hrs.	• Have a date night with my spouse. • Take the kids to the park (with no "agenda"). • Have dinner together every night this week.
Having Fun	☐ Yes ☑ No	5 hrs.	• Activities: golf, skiing, cooking class • Learn a new joke and tell it to somebody. • Time with friends: movies, dinner party
Creating Career Excellence	☐ Yes ☑ No	2 hrs.	• Take the training course I've been putting off. • Reward those around me who have contributed to my success. • Find a coach/mentor.
Serving Others	☐ Yes ☑ No	2 hrs.	• Sign up to be a youth mentor. • Volunteer for a church committee. • Participate in the Walk-a-thon for M.S.

you know what you need to do to experience them—and you realize there are only a finite number of hours in the day—the decision to delegate what you can is easy. Nobody wastes a life days, weeks, months, or years at a time. It's fifteen minutes here . . . a half-hour there . . . a few hours occasionally . . . that are easily wasted. I strongly encourage you to consider delegating what you can and focusing your time and energy on what's important to you. Maybe you can find time for some of the activities you include on your Quality of Life Enhancer Worksheet by delegating your financial affairs.

To complete your own worksheet, turn to page 87 or 88. Either using the same "Life Qualities" as I've provided in the sample on page 83 or substituting your own list, fill in the left column first. Then check yes or no under the "Delegatable?" column, determine how many hours a week you'd like to spend on these qualities, and choose a few specific activities you'd do. So often we make choices about how we'll spend our time unconsciously, and this worksheet is designed to help you make conscious choices.

Author Wayne Dyer is famous for writing about his work with people with terminal illnesses. Perhaps his most quotable remark has been that none of those people, confronted with their final days, said they wished they'd spent more time in the office. It's hard to imagine that they would have said they wished they'd spent more time reading financial magazines, surfing financial Web sites, and checking their stock performance, either.

What about you? Dyer's point was that if you wouldn't choose to squander your last week, why would you throw away *any* of your time? Financial wisdom could be defined as being able to distinguish between what the media, financial companies, and economic information sources try to convince us is absolutely critical from what *actually contributes to having a great life.*

Here are some things to consider:

- ❑ Do you know what a P/E ratio is but not an HDL/LDL ratio?

- ❑ Do you know how many stars your mutual fund has, but have no idea about your body fat percentage?

- ❑ Are you more likely to read *Money* magazine this week than the Bible, the Koran, or some other great spiritual text?

- ❑ Will you spend more time this week watching financial shows on TV than meditating or praying?

- ❑ Did you sign more proxy cards for your stocks and mutual funds than birthday cards for your friends and family?

- ❑ Will you spend more time connected to the Internet than to your friends, children, spouse, or parents?

- ❑ Do you check your investments daily but not floss daily? (I know that seems silly, but I recently read that if you floss every day, you can add 6.5 years to your life.)

Since we don't know what we don't know, it's possible that you're not even aware of how much better your life would be with a shift in how you spend your time. If there's one thing I absolutely want to get across to you in this chapter, it is that if spending time on your finances is drawing you away from what is really most important, seek help. In the next few chapters you will learn how to discern the difference between legitimate financial advisors and those who are just product salespeople. So don't allow any uncertainty you may have about where or how to find an advisor get in the way of a healthy assessment of whether you ought to seek one.

What's next?

Look again at your Financial Road Map. If it's still blank, you probably *need* some help. If your Financial Road Map is complete, you may *want* help creating and implementing a strategy. If you've decided you are a Do-it-yourselfer, you must begin educating yourself. Start by reviewing the Web site summarized in the sidebar on pages 66–69 to get a complete picture of all the subjects you need to master. Then I suggest you begin to methodically check each of them off your list. Attend seminars, read books, amass a list of reliable online sources. Basically, it's off to school for you to become a truly competent Do-it-yourselfer.

If, on the other hand, you are a Collaborator or Delegator, you have a different kind of research to conduct. It will be less time consuming by far, but no less important. You must find yourself a Trusted Advisor.

The Quality of Life Enhancer Worksheet™

NAME: _____

Life Quality	Delegatable?	More Hours Per Week I'd Like to Spend on This	What are three activities I would do this week to improve this area of my life?
	☐ Yes ☐ No		
	☐ Yes ☐ No		
	☐ Yes ☐ No		
	☐ Yes ☐ No		
	☐ Yes ☐ No		
	☐ Yes ☐ No		

The Quality of Life Enhancer Worksheet™

NAME: _____

Life Quality	Delegatable?	More Hours Per Week I'd Like to Spend on This	What are three activities I would do this week to improve this area of my life?
	☐ Yes ☐ No		
	☐ Yes ☐ No		
	☐ Yes ☐ No		
	☐ Yes ☐ No		
	☐ Yes ☐ No		
	☐ Yes ☐ No		

CHAPTER 6

FIND A TRUSTED ADVISOR AND AVOID SALESPEOPLE: IDENTIFYING THE 3 TYPES OF FINANCIAL PROFESSIONALS

> *Listen to a man's words and look at the pupil of his eye. How can a man conceal his character?*
>
> MENCIUS
> *Works* (Fourth–Third Century B.C.)

If you're going to disclose your entire financial picture, including your values, goals, assets and liabilities—and delegate the creation and implementation of a tailored financial plan—you want to work with someone you can trust.

Someone who is both competent and caring, professional and proficient. Someone who wants more than to sell you a mutual fund, an insurance policy, or investment management services. Someone you can count on to keep the big picture in mind, the needs of you and your loved ones foremost, and the details of your personal finances confidential. What you want is a Trusted Advisor.

"Trusted Advisor" is a term I've trademarked to describe the kinds of financial professionals who come to me for coaching—the kind of people who are interested in taking their businesses to the next level of value and meaning for their clients. They attend my seminars and listen to my audiotapes out of a desire to find and serve people who want a relationship with an expert rather than a transaction with a salesperson. Of course, being a Trusted Advisor requires more than learning a certain set of skills or adopting a new level of professionalism; it means that the advisor has to actually earn and maintain the trust of clients.

If you were given this book by a financial advisor, it was probably his or her intent to provide you additional insights into what you should expect in your working relationship. This chapter is likely to reinforce your decision to work with that person. If, on the other hand, you came to this book some other way, and you've decided that you are or want to be a Delegator, then this chapter will help you find a Trusted Advisor.

In your search for the right person, you may encounter three types of individuals: the "scientific" salesperson, the so-called consultant (who is actually a salesperson pretending to be a financial planner), and the genuine article: the trustworthy and competent advisor. It's unfortunate that they don't hang out a shingle to let us know which group they fall into. Their titles are no indication, either.

Stockbroker, insurance agent, financial planner, financial advisor, financial consultant, estate counselor, CFP, CFS, CIMC, CLU, ChFC: none of these labels is a clue. Neither is the big-name company they might represent. So you must assess each individual based on a set of characteristics and, ideally, recommendations from a friend, family member, or another advisor. The Trusted Advisor rarely advertises, makes cold calls, or direct markets, so you are most likely to find one by referral.

CHARACTERISTICS OF SALESPEOPLE AND TRUSTED ADVISORS

What do the salespeople in most used-car lots, some appliance and shoe stores, and all telemarketers who call during our dinnertime have in common? They make us cringe because of their sales methods. We have come to expect any interaction with these people to leave us feeling put off by their rabid insistence on never taking no for an answer.

The bad news is that some people in the financial industry have been trained in the old-fashioned manipulation methods; many of them can persuade us with more subtle tactics, but they're still tactics, nonetheless. For a lot of them, it's just the training they got, or advice handed down from one generation to the next. There are plenty of nice, honest, hard-working people who work for companies whose training methods are more than thirty years old.

There are also those salespeople who are so product-focused that they don't spend much time thinking about the people who buy from them. One young couple of Do-it-yourselfers I know figured out the specific kind of life insurance they needed based on the research they'd done and their assessment of short- and long-term goals. The woman contacted a reputable agent to make the purchase. Without knowing anything about this couple's finances, the agent told her, "No, that's not what you want. Here's the product you want." Of course, this product was more expensive and, to be fair, a better investment. But the couple didn't want the insurance as an investment, and while the product might be "superior" in a vacuum, it did not fit with this couple's big picture.

Rather than get in an argument about the merits of different kinds of life insurance, the woman firmly stated that their goals dictated a specific kind of insurance purchase. Was the salesperson willing to sell them that product? Yes, he was. Because the couple had educated themselves and done the groundwork to understand their values and goals, this was a minor annoyance and not a major derailment. But, as a Delegator, you can see how working with salespeople who are less interested in your future than in today's sale would be a big mistake.

What's the good news? There are plenty of financial professionals who have moved on from those transaction-oriented sales techniques (or who never employed them) and are more concerned with client-centered practices.

David Bach, the author of the book *Smart Women Finish Rich* and an exemplary Trusted Advisor, enjoyed telling me the story of a man who came to make a stock purchase from him. The fellow came in, requested a $10,000 transaction, and was floored when David told him that he couldn't do the deal.

"Why not?" the man asked.

"Well, I don't do that," David said.

Perplexed, the man looked around David's office. "What do you mean, you 'don't do that'? Where am I? I'm at a brokerage firm, right?"

"Yes," David smiled. "You can buy that from someone else here, but you can't do it with me. I work differently."

"Well . . . what the heck do *you* do?"

David told him that he was in the business of preparing comprehensive plans, that he wanted to know what was important to this man, to plot his goals and financial picture on a Financial Road Map, and then come up with a strategy that would fit with his overall game plan—not just help him make a random purchase because the man thought it was a good idea that day.

Although the man was surprised that David wouldn't just take his money, he was also intrigued by this different way of doing things. He happened to have all of his financial documents because he had grabbed the file to make the purchase, so they proceeded right then and there with a Values Conversation, goals prioritization, financial review, and creating a Financial Road Map. This man became one of David's most grateful clients because he'd had almost a million dollars scattered in more than fifteen accounts. Today, he receives a consolidated statement instead of multiple statements throughout the month, he makes financial decisions based on a comprehensive strategy, and he has David as his Trusted Advisor. This man hadn't known that such advisors existed, but once he did, he recognized this was the way to go for him.

You can see that it's incredibly easy to spot a Trusted Advisor when you encounter one. It's also easy to spot the salespeople and avoid them once you know their underlying objectives and principles. In this chapter, I'll share with you the surefire methods for telling right away exactly who you're dealing with. I'll also give you some tips for determining whether you are talking to someone who is merely competent, or someone who is also trustworthy.

The following chart outlines the essential differences between salespeople and Trusted Advisors. Keep these in mind as you meet potential advisors. The most basic distinction is that salespeople are looking for a need to fill—and they want to fill it no matter what. They try to identify *one* of your financial needs and sell you a product to satisfy that need. They tend to ask what they call "probing questions": Have you ever been asked something that made you feel like you were being backed into a corner, and your only way out was to buy the product? Salespeople also call this "digging you a hole and throwing you a rope." The follow-up they do is intended to sell you other products to meet other needs until they get most or all of your financial business. They also call it "dripping" on you. (Pleasant metaphor, don't you think?) They point out pain and problems, try to make you uncomfortable, and motivate you to buy more, contact them, or respond when they call.

"The main reason I decided to invest with George, my Trusted Advisor, is that the Financial Road Map really inspired me. When George took me down 'the road,' he recognized what was truly important in my life and he was able to tailor my financial investments to help me reach my personal goals and aspirations. The experience of my Financial Road Map was incredible!"

Becky Lathrop
Business Consultant • West Palm, Florida

In contrast, Trusted Advisors will not sell you *anything* before they see your *whole* financial picture: this means all of your financial information. So if you refuse to show them everything, they will refuse to work with you. At first, the salesperson's approach may sound more service-oriented or even more rational: "Let's just take care of one thing at a time . . . .". But it's not. Just as your skeleton, muscles, nervous system, and cardiovascular system are interdependent, so are the various aspects of your financial life. A real pro will not allow you to relegate him or her to working with only partial understanding; this would be like a doctor who makes diagnoses and writes prescriptions without a full examination and family history. You can find doctors like that, but is this who you'd want to entrust with your health?

Trusted Advisor	Salesperson
• Has a structured process for creating a comprehensive financial plan for clients and can tell you what it is.	• Has a technique for making the sale.
• Is interested in what's important to you and wants to listen to your significant issues in the first meeting.	• Engages you in small talk, chitchat, or banter designed to relax you and establish rapport with you. ("How long have you lived in the area?" "What's your favorite sports team?")
• Requires that you bring all of your financial data to the first meeting, but does not require that you disclose any information until you are comfortable.	• Does not require that you do anything other than show up to the first meeting. Asks probing, personal questions designed to make you uncomfortable.
• Expresses interest in and refers frequently to the work you have done to prepare for the first meeting, including your Financial Road Map, in an effort to understand you.	• Refers frequently to your impending demise, the need to protect your family, and so on, in an attempt to scare you into buying a product to fill a need.
• Is happy to refer you to someone else if he or she senses there is not a good match.	• Will tell you that he or she can (and will) work with anybody.

Trusted Advisor	Salesperson
• Meets with you in a professional environment and requires that anyone who shares financial decisions and responsibilities be present.	• Will meet with anyone, anywhere, anytime in the name of "convenience"; however, this is a sign of desperation.
• Inspires you in a positive way.	• Tends to prey on your fears and insecurities to get you to buy.
• Won't be talked into just selling you a product even if you insist.	• Will sell you anything you want to buy, or will simply redirect you to a preferred product.

The Evolution of Sales

Confession: I am a reformed salesperson. I was thoroughly trained in and have used the sales techniques described in this chapter. They worked, and I was highly productive.

When I was a financial advisor, I went through a popular sales course that met once a week. During the last week of the course, there were several award contests, among them the "Sales Talk Champion" contest where we stood in front of the room, glibly using persuasion techniques we had learned.

At our awards ceremony, they announced, "And the Sales Talk Champion is . . . Bill Bachrach!" They handed me a plaque and asked me to share a few words.

continued on next page

This was a pivotal moment for me. My mind went blank as I started thinking, *Where do I hang a plaque that dubs me the Sales Talk Champion?* The easier question is, *Where wouldn't I hang it?* (Can you imagine walking into someone's office with a Sales Talk Champion plaque hanging on the wall and trusting them with your money?) I mumbled something and tried to be gracious, then got out of the limelight quickly. I was thinking, *There's no way I can hang this up anywhere.* I realized I was becoming someone I didn't want to be. I didn't want to be great at handling objections and closing skills. I didn't want to be a Sales Talk Champion.

Now, I look back on this "learning experience" with mild embarrassment. Like many financial professionals, I eventually matured and evolved, both in my career and in my thinking, to a more sophisticated view about doing business.

Likewise, the entire financial product-vending process has undergone an evolution of its own. For expediency, we'll call it the "evolution of sales," since it traces in broad strokes the predominant method of working with customers. A colleague of mine, Doug Carter, described this as the "Seven Generations of Selling"; what follows is my interpretation of his idea.

These seven steps, which have taken place over hundreds of years and can also evolve in one individual, have been dictated primarily by the availability of goods and the proximity of buyers. Following are those steps, presented here so you can instantly recognize the kind of marketing mind-set you are dealing with when you interview potential advisors.

First Generation—Barter, or *trade*, is the one-for-one exchange of goods between two people: "I'll trade you this animal pelt for that club."

Second Generation—A *merchant* is someone who stocks up on various items garnered through trade, then makes that stock available to others from one location, such as a trading post. Buyers bring items to trade or use a medium of exchange, such as conch shells or, later, currency. (You're not likely to find many financial pros bartering or acting as merchants, but we've included it here to give you the whole picture.)

Third Generation—The *peddler* takes his "store" on the road to hock his wares to new customers in new locations. This wandering vendor was the first "pitchman." The pitchman (or pitchwoman) is alive and well among the insurance agents who make house calls and the stockbrokers who make cold calls.

Fourth Generation—When the peddler discovered the profit in repeat business, he began to follow a *route*. If you have a newspaper delivered on your doorstep or products delivered through the mail on a regular basis, you are a customer along the modern route. The financial product salesperson who prevails on you to buy one product to fill a need, then "drips" on you with a newsletter and follows up later so you buy something else, is likewise a peddler. The Collaborator is a stop on the financial services peddler's route.

Fifth Generation—The *"scientific" approach* began in the 1930s with organized sales training. Sayings like "find a need

continued on next page

and fill it" define this generation of selling. The underlying idea is that salespeople can find prospects who lack a benefit the product provides and, by pointing out that lack, convince them to buy it.

To be successful, the salespeople have to learn how to endure and "handle" objections, never take no for an answer, and generally make pests of themselves. Persistence is highly regarded and rewarded. For the Generation Five salesperson, creating customers is a numbers game.

This is where scripts and memorization began. Negative emotions like fear, greed, or guilt dominate this approach. The objective of the salesperson is to create pain or focus on a problem to motivate the prospect to buy. Fifth generation salespeople try to appeal to greed. "You're only getting x percent? Our money managers get y." This is the level where most of the financial industry has been trained and remains stuck. They conduct a "needs analysis" to see what products you should buy, then apply pressure until you cave in or flee the scene. To prey on your fears, they use "disturbing questions" about paying too much tax, outliving your money in retirement, losing buying power to inflation, becoming disabled, or dying prematurely. The purpose is to create discomfort so they can manipulate your behavior.

Sixth Generation—Then came the *consultative approach.* It sounds better, yet Generation Six is just Generation Five in sheep's clothing. Along the way, someone noticed that people would rather buy from a person they like, so "rapport building" was studied and learned like some elaborate magic trick. The theory: Become their buddy and they are more likely to buy. Most "relationship" selling models propose the illusion of a relationship that doesn't really exist to avoid the impression of manipulation. But what's more manipulative than pretending to be somebody's friend just to get some business?

How does it work? The salespeople/counselors initiate superficial chitchat to find some "common ground" to create feelings of rapport. Then they launch into a series of "probing" questions to back you into a corner. The objective: to make sure your only way out is to buy the product they propose as the "solution."

Rather than an honest interview to determine if there is a basis for a business relationship, the "consultant" makes a presentation punctuated by questions. In other words, the only reason questions are asked is to create the false impression that the process is interactive. The real purpose of the questions is so the salesperson knows which presentation to make to sell the products he or she wants to sell.

Generations Five and Six dominate the current landscape. Most financial professionals you meet have been trained this way. The primary motive is still to sell a specific product, and the information is gathered for that purpose alone. You may think you've met someone with your best interests in mind, but it's usually hocus pocus, smoke and mirrors, not truly consultative at all.

continued on next page

Seventh Generation—The Trusted Advisor's process features discovery. He or she acts as facilitator to help potential clients discover what's important to them, articulate their goals, and benchmark where they are now. This discovery *on the part of the prospective client* sets the tone for a healthy business relationship to naturally and rapidly develop. The Trusted Advisor is free to recommend the best course of action, which may be an advisor-client relationship, a referral to a transaction-oriented salesperson, or no action whatsoever. The client's discovery of the truth in a positive, enlightening manner tends to instill a strong resolve to take action right away.

Trusted Advisors never appeal to your negative emotions, such as fear or greed, to sell. Instead, they choose to inspire you to make the best choices so you can have the kind of life you want. They understand that the vast majority of people would rather do business with someone who inspires them than someone who scares them.

And although they are neither cavalier nor arrogant, you have a sense that the Trusted Advisor is not trying to convince you, persuade you, or sell you—and can take or leave your money.

SCREENING BY PHONE

One sign that you're talking to a scientific salesperson or so-called consultant is that he or she has all the time in the world to chat. A Trusted Advisor's time is precious and you need to respect it, but you are entitled to ask a few questions.

Ideally, you will say something like this:

> *Hi, my name is Terry Smith. My colleague, Dale Jones, suggested that I contact you because I am ready to engage a financial advisor. My financial situation is similar in some ways to Dale's, so we may be a good fit.*
>
> *I know your time is valuable, and so is mine, so I'm hoping we can have about a ten-minute phone conversation to determine whether or not we should meet.*

[If the advisor agrees, you can proceed. If not, schedule a time that works for both of you.]

> *What do you need to know from me to determine if I am a possible fit for your services?*

[Trusted Advisors tend to have standards or specialize in helping similar types of people. If you closely match the description the advisor provides, continue. If not, politely end the conversation and try again with someone else. Expect the advisor to talk about personality, financial standing, and other specifics. For example, a Trusted Advisor would say, "We specialize in helping people who ————, and who meet these specific criteria." If your potential advisor can't answer the question ("Gee, I don't know,") or won't answer the question ("That's not really important. Tell me about yourself . . .") you're talking to a salesperson.]

What do you require from us in a first meeting?

[Really good advisors will expect you to come to their offices, carry all your financial documents, and bring your partner.]

My next question is about your process. What would be the steps we'd take in our first meeting?

[If you are satisfied with the answer, continue. Again, if the person can't or won't answer the question, you are dealing with a salesperson.] *I've just finished working through a book called* Values-Based Financial Planning *to prepare for our meeting. I'd like to bring the materials, such as a Financial Road Map, that I've created to help facilitate the conversation. If that's okay with you, let's schedule a time to get together and decide if we are a good match.*

[Assuming you may have a good match, the advisor should express enthusiasm for a meeting, request that you (and your spouse or partner, if you have one) come to his or her office with all of your financial data in hand, and set an appointment, then hang up.]

If at any time during this phone call the person tries to engage you in a conversation about your financial information, or fails to request your financial information at the time of your first meeting, you guessed it—salesperson. You can and should back out at any point in the phone call when you see a red flag. It'll be time lost but not wasted.

Once you've found someone who can answer these questions to your satisfaction, asks you questions that seem appropriate, and has standards that impress you, you are ready for a first meeting. Plan to take the worksheets you've done in this book, your financial information, and an inquisitive attitude.

In the next chapter, you'll learn the final steps in determining if you have found your Trusted Advisor. You're on the home stretch!

CHAPTER 7

INTERVIEW POTENTIAL ADVISORS: TESTING THE TRUSTWORTHINESS AND COMPETENCE OF A FINANCIAL PROFESSIONAL

Winning is not complicated.
People complicate it.
If you surround yourself with
the right people, you win.

DICK VERMEIL
general manager and football coach of the
Super Bowl XXXIV champions, St. Louis Rams

L et's say that John Elway—in the prime of his football career as quarterback of the Denver Broncos—stepped into a huddle and nobody knew who he was. Do you think the players would be able to spot his expertise anyway?

Even though this would never happen, play along for a minute. The team would know right off, wouldn't they? He would not have to tell them, "Look, you guys, before I call the play, you probably want to know a little about who I am and what my background is. I know none of you have heard of me because there was some kind of NFL amnesia virus going around, but I've got two Super Bowl rings, and I am the ultimate, last-minute, comeback guy. I can take us down the field in the fourth quarter with almost no time left and be better than anybody who ever played the game."

Instead, all he'd have to do is walk into the huddle, *be* John Elway—a truly great quarterback—take charge, and tell them what to do. They'd get an inkling, don't you think? That instinct would lead them to execute the play as instructed, and when Elway delivered, they'd still be in awe.

People who are great in any field don't have to spell it out. You can tell by potential advisors' behavior and demeanor whether they are good at what they do. A Trusted Advisor would simply walk into the new client meeting, *be* himself or herself—a true pro—ask the right questions, and always operate at the highest standards. You'd know whether you were talking to the first string or a benchwarmer. Like John Elway, a Trusted Advisor's competence level and trustworthiness are demonstrated by behavior and backed up by delivery.

As you seek the right advisor for you, don't get too distracted by designations or tenure in the financial services industry. Designations may be reassuring, but they don't *really* mean an advisor is any better at this business than someone who doesn't have them. The best Certified Financial Planners, for example, know other CFPs whom they would never trust with their own money. Similarly, the number of years in the business has little to do with actual competence.

Maturity has its advantages—wisdom gained from life lessons, sometimes a stronger sense of self and direction, a parental warmth (for younger clients), or a sense of shared experiences (for older clients)—yet someone once said that few people actually have twenty years of experience; instead, most people have one year of experience twenty times. Younger or newer advisors may be more technologically adept and fresher to the game. But you have to be careful about generalizing; there are plenty of computer-savvy advisors over fifty, and there are an equal number of wise thirty-year-olds.

The size of the firm that employs them is no indication, either. Bigger companies may provide better training, but that training could be Generation Five or Six sales techniques. Some companies will provide access to a lot of resources, expertise, and experience, but the Internet has equalized the playing field: even an independent advisor has ready access to all the resources the big firms used to control.

My point is this: You have to rely on your gut reaction to the individual you're meeting and use certain other criteria (see the checklist at the end of this chapter) as a backup. You simply want to find an advisor who inspires your trust and who has followed the BRG ("being really good") formula for success. It goes back to the Elway analogy. *You know when you are in the presence of a pro.* There should be no doubt in your mind.

An interview with the right advisor will be such a profound experience for you that after about an hour you will feel ready to hire the advisor to write your financial plan, trust him or her with all your money, stop working with any other advisors, do whatever this advisor tells you to do, and share the good news with your friends, family, and colleagues about the incredible experience you had. When you meet with a Trusted Advisor, you feel energized. In contrast, when you meet with a salesperson, you feel worn down.

When the meeting is over, ask yourself, *Do I feel inspired?*

The Trusted Advisor has also mastered a certain paradox: how to care about you yet be detached enough to say when there isn't a good fit or you have mistaken ideas about how to proceed. It's one part "tough love" and one part caring more about doing good business than making money for themselves.

Look to find a great advisor, not just one who wants your business. You should have a sense that your advisor cares about you as a person, but could take or leave your money. Eagerness is not a plus in this profession; you really want to stay away from the person who seems hungry or over-enthusiastic. You also want a financially successful advisor. After all, who wants an advisor who's broke? That's like having an obese, cigarette-smoking fitness instructor. This is your financial future; don't entrust it to someone who is so zealous to please you that his or her judgment is swayed by that desire. Instead, look for someone who has the confidence to tell you the truth whether it's what you want to hear or not, guide you as you work toward your financial goals, and support you in fulfilling your values.

THE ADVISOR SHOULD INTERVIEW YOU, NOT THE OTHER WAY AROUND

Prior to your meeting, a Trusted Advisor will not only request but will require that certain things occur. If the advisor does not insist on any of these, you should question the wisdom of proceeding with this person.

1. Both partners (if you are not single) attend the first meeting to make sure there is a good "fit" with *everyone* involved.

2. You bring all of your financial documents to this meeting. You may elect not to share them if you decide this is not the right advisor for you, but you should be prepared.

3. You meet in his or her office, not at a restaurant, your home, or any other venue.

When you get to the meeting, you can take one of two tacks with your potential advisor: either "here I am" or "show me." The here-I-am approach leads with full disclosure: "I'm here because I don't want to spend all my time managing my money. I've completed a number of exercises to help figure out what's important to me, my precise goals, and my current financial situation. I have all of that information with me. How do you want to get started?" On the other hand, if you're a skeptic, you may be more comfortable with the show-me approach: "Hi, it's nice to meet you. Why don't you show me how you work?" You can then simply participate and wait to see if the advisor will call for all that you've brought with you.

"The initial interview utilizing the 'road map' approach was very helpful in identifying my lifestyle goals, from my immediate needs to month-to-month (college expenses, house maintenance, etc.) to my retirement needs since the death of my husband. This initial interview process also gave me excellent opportunity to begin assessing the strategy that my advisor would be setting up to manage my future finances."

Ann E. Miller
Medical Technologist • Richmond, Kentucky

If you're dealing with a Trusted Advisor, either approach should ultimately elicit the same response, which is a series of pointed questions to first help the advisor get to know what's important to you, then prioritize and define your goals, and finally benchmark your current financial situation. If you're going the here-I-am route, it may be delayed slightly as the advisor gives you a surprised look (not many people are this prepared or this forthright), pleasantly asks to see what you've brought, then gives it due attention. But it should end up in the same place: the advisor should ask questions and listen a whole lot more than talk.

Don't be surprised if he or she wants to audiotape or videotape your meeting. This is an excellent technique that allows the advisor to be both detail-oriented and attentive to you at the same time. Have you ever watched a movie a second or third time and caught things you didn't see the first time? That's why good advisors might listen to or view the tape several times: to make sure the strategy they create and the advice they give are absolutely the best for you. This isn't a sign of weakness or an inability to remember; it's a sign of thoroughness and commitment to do the best possible job for you.

Every single item you've created while reading this book should be addressed. It may not be requested in exactly the same form as you've learned here, but it should be obvious to you that the advisor is following the same principles. You will also be able to learn a lot about the advisor by observing how he or she listens to you. This is one advantage of attending the first meeting with a partner. While you're talking about your values or goals or financial material, your partner can be watching the advisor, noting any impatience or "going through the motions," looking for the Trusted Advisor's signature attentiveness, genuine caring, and thorough documentation of your answers.

You should know that a good advisor will be evaluating you, too. The Trusted Advisor has standards, ideal client profiles, and not everyone who wants to hire the Trusted Advisor will be invited to do so. He or she will be assessing whether you are the kind of person who can be genuinely helped by the services he or she offers. In the advisor's mind, you may be classified in several ways: personality, net worth, financial objectives, and so on.

What Kind of Client Will You Be?

There are financial advisors for just about every financial situation. Some prefer to work only with people who have high net worths, others are more interested in helping young couples get established, and there are still others who work with all kinds of people in between.

While smart clients are getting better at selecting an advisor, smart advisors are also getting better at selecting their clients. Following are four client types. Of course, they are generalizations, so not everyone will fit perfectly into one of the categories, but you should find this useful. The categories of clients (which could probably be applied to any kind of service business) are included to give you perspective on the Trusted Advisor's screening process. They're not intended to teach you how to appear as if you're the right client for a Trusted Advisor; that would be counterproductive. But they should help you understand how the top professionals serve their clients by

continued on next page

taking on only those they *know* they can serve well. This is your opportunity to see yourself through the eyes of an advisor. Chances are, if you've read this far and done the exercises, you're just the kind of client a Trusted Advisor wants.

1. The Great Client.

Great clients are coachable and financially responsible. They want to manage their money intelligently. These people are receptive to dealing with a financial professional because their time is precious and they like having business relationships. They are busy working on their own career success, running a business or, as happy retirees, doing what they enjoy. Because Great Clients are good at their own professions, they respect others who also excel.

Great Clients recognize the importance of finding someone who is trustworthy, competent, and knowledgeable to help them with their financial choices. They see the whole process of creating a financial strategy as exciting and important. They get excellent value for their money because they follow the advice they pay for and implement the plans to get them where they want to go.

Great Clients are not pushovers or "lay downs." They are just straightforward and sincere, and they don't play games.

They are people the advisor genuinely cares about, who require a valuable service, and whose trust the advisor holds as a privilege and foundation of the relationship.

2. People who are fun but financially hopeless.

These charmers are great to socialize with because they love spending their money. Unfortunately, these genuinely nice people make lousy clients for Trusted Advisors, no matter how much money they earn. If only they could invest as well as they rationalize ("You live only once!" "You can't take it with you!" "Money can't buy happiness!"), they would be very, very rich.

A few people like this might become Great Clients at some point, perhaps when they're fifty-five years old and realize they have only ten years to save for retirement. For now, they are reluctant to share the details of their financial conditions and are embarrassed about past financial choices. They are smart enough to know they are digging their own financial graves, but lack the discipline to change their "fatal" habits. They may be cavalier about their financial futures because of expected inheritances or benefactors. They rarely get their financial documents together, no matter how important they understand it to be. Essentially, people who are fun but financially hopeless think having a good excuse for not getting their financial lives together is as good as having a sound financial strategy.

3. People who use advisors for information.

These people have the discipline to manage their own money, and they enjoy doing research. They use financial professionals for information, and then they buy their investments or insurance from the cheapest source. They believe this approach is perfectly legitimate. They may have such low opinions of financial professionals that they have no qualms at all about taking advantage of them. ("Well, if this idiot is willing to take me out to lunch just on the off-chance of getting my business, I'll let him.")

Ethics aside, the primary downside of this approach is that the information gleaned from "using" is generally not of the highest caliber. It's unlikely that someone who uses advisors for information will have much to do with a Trusted Advisor, simply because a Trusted Advisor guards against spending time with someone like this.

4. People who don't trust anybody.

These lonely souls always expect to be betrayed. In their minds, danger lurks around the next corner. They have a litany of bad business and relationship experiences. They think that trusting other people is naïve and foolish. Whatever psychological difficulties these people may have, financial professionals aren't qualified to provide the kind of counseling they need.

Assuming that you are a Great Client or on your way to becoming one, you want to find an advisor who will work *only* with Great Clients because

- other types suck the life out of an advisor's business, leaving less time and energy for great clients,

- advisors who are willing to put up with the other three kinds of clients are either too eager or too green for you, and

- advisors who will take all comers are not advisors at all; they are salespeople.

HOW ARE FINANCIAL PROFESSIONALS PAID?

For the financial services industry, the recent decades have brought massive, lightning-quick consolidation and completely changed the rules of the game. Even the term *financial services* didn't exist before the 1980s.

In the past, financial professionals worked mostly on commission, just like appliance or car salespeople. Yet today, many are turning to fee-based compensation because it is, in most cases, in better alignment with the business model of a valued consultant. Although the way your advisor is compensated is not a sole determinant in answering the salesperson versus Trusted Advisor question, it can give you insight into how the advisor thinks about his or her business.

Your advisor will probably bring up the issue of payment before you have to ask. Expect to learn the percentage earned on each transaction, or the fees charged to write a plan and manage your money. Negotiation should be out of the question; if the person suggests the price may be "flexible," you could be dealing with a car-sales mentality and not the kind of advisor you need to manage your finances. Most Trusted Advisors have predetermined rates based on your assets and/or the services provided.

As in most business arrangements, you are going to pay for what you get and probably get what you pay for. You are likely to encounter the following types of fee arrangements:

- hourly compensation;
- flat annual fee;

- a fee to create the written plan, plus a percentage of assets for ongoing services;
- no fee for plan, but commissions for implementing the plan for you; and
- fee for initial services, plus commissions on additional transactions.

Personally, I am fond of the fee-based system. I figure that the annual amount paid is a fair share of the ongoing work an advisor does to stay knowledgeable about the issues that affect your money. It's what you pay for having someone in your life to think about you and your family and to meet with you on a regular basis to discuss your concerns and opportunities. That ongoing fee is a small price to pay to be able to telephone someone whenever you want to talk about your financial issues or to access one of the trusted professionals in his or her network for accounting work, legal work, or to refinance your mortgage.

What You Can Expect from Your Trusted Advisor

At the beginning of your relationship with an advisor, you will have disclosed some very personal information, including your entire financial picture and what's most important to you. Once you've selected this advisor to work with you to create a plan for your financial future, you will be investing much more than money; you will be investing your trust.

What should you expect in return?

First and foremost, you should expect excellence: competence and thoroughness in preparing your plan, professionalism in presenting it to you, guidance in implementing it, and regular follow-up to monitor your progress toward your financial goals.

You will know that your advisor has done a good job in preparing your plan when the following occur.

❑ Everything you've talked about has been taken into consideration. It is obvious that the advisor listened to you and constructed a plan based on what you discussed.

❑ You feel compelled to take action. The plan is understandable, doable, and inspiring.

❑ The plan is clearly tailored to *your* values and goals—but the advisor makes recommendations based on his or her expertise, too. For example, risk tolerance can be a slippery issue. If you said you felt comfortable seeking x percent return on your investments, but your advisor realized that you need to seek y percent to reach your goals, the advisor explains this and suggests strategies.

With the plan in hand, you have one crucial job: Implement it. You may have to purchase recommended financial products, allocate assets based on the advice, adjust your insurance as indicated, start a cash savings plan, manage your debt in a new way, and take care of some legal matter, such as a will, trust, or other estate planning. Once you've accomplished these tasks (usually with the advisor's help), the hard work is done, but your relationship is really just beginning. *This is when the advisor becomes most valuable to you.* Now you get to stop thinking about your money!

This is not to say that you wash your hands of financial responsibility. It merely means that now it's the advisor's job to schedule regular meetings to apprise you of your overall progress toward your goals, to check in to see if any of those goals have changed, and to inspire you to stay the course, insulating you from financial pornography and well-meaning people who create doubt about your chosen path.

The best advisors help you stay focused on what really matters through two essential, value-added services: updating your financial organizer and preparing a special kind of report that totals all of your assets and measures progress toward your goals.

1. The Financial Organizer. You've already gathered all of your financial documents to build a plan, so the natural next step for your advisor is to organize them in a way that creates quickest and easiest access to the information. Top advisors have a standardized system for this organization. Their goal is to simplify their clients' financial lives and give them security that they are in good hands.

This financial organizer can take many forms—maybe it's a three-ring binder or an accordion file—but it should contain all essential financial information, including statements, summaries, or other documentation. The objective is to make assessing the status of each of these as easy as possible. You'll recognize this list from chapter 3, "Benchmark Your Current Financial Reality: Gathering Your Documents":

- Income: tax returns
- Retirement plan: company, 401(k), Keogh, SEP, IRA, RRSP, TSA, or other statements
- CDs and savings accounts: bank statements, money market fund statements
- Brokerage account holdings: stocks (and stock options), bonds, mutual fund statements

- Insurance: summaries of life, disability, health, long-term care policies, annuities, etc.

- Real estate: appraisals of the primary residence, vacation homes, investment property

- Collectibles: appraisals of precious metals, art, or others

- Business: owners' balance sheets, profit-and-loss statements, and appraisals or business valuations

- Expected inheritance

The filing system should be simple and clearly labeled (as easy to maintain as to access), so that either you can update it monthly as statements arrive, or else it is a quick job for one of the advisor's staff members to complete just prior to a meeting. The advisor can either keep only the current statements in the organizer, or purge it once a year.

For your convenience, it should also include any estate planning documents, such as wills, trusts, even advance medical directives and powers of attorney. Ultimately, the organizer should identify the value of everything you own, available in one place for you to get a complete, concise financial picture.

2. The Progress-Measuring Report. If you ask most people what the aggregate return has been on their financial investments, they have to resort to quoting figures they remember from one statement or another. They can talk about some aspect of their financial standing, but they don't really see the big picture. They have people in their lives claiming to be financial advisors, but they can't answer this simple question: What was the total return on your entire portfolio last year and for this year to date?

Your Trusted Advisor *must* provide you with this information.

He or she will take all the information from your various statements, consolidated and otherwise, and create the mother of all consolidated statements: a report that shows the total value of everything you own, from the worth of a rare stamp collection to the cash value on a life insurance policy to those assets actually on deposit with the companies the advisor represents. This report will include the value of *everything* in the financial organizer.

With this kind of statement, you can expect your advisor to say to you, "When we began, you started out with x. By the beginning of this year, you had already grown to y. Based on our projections, you're on track to meet your goal by the year 2010. The aggregate growth of your wealth for this year is z percent."

This is the most valuable information your advisor can provide you. Who cares about the performance of one stock or mutual fund, which may fluctuate from year to year, if you are working toward goals that require a five-, ten-, or twenty-year plan? Who cares about ups and downs of bonds when you are working on a *comprehensive* financial picture? You and your advisor should stay focused on and talk about what's important: How well are you progressing along the road you've mapped out? Are you on track to meet your milestones (goals)? Is this plan actually helping you fulfill your values? If not, where do adjustments need to be made?

You want your advisor to be regularly thinking and communicating with you about these matters. Sure, advisors need to stay on top of individual performance to assess whether adjustments need to be made in someone's strategy, but *let them worry about performance on their own time.* Don't let them waste your time with tales of market woe or glory. You have only one question: *Am I on track to achieve my goals?*

The Trusted Advisor Checklist

❏ **If you heard of the advisor by referral, did he or she receive a strong recommendation?** Perhaps the best indicator, the recommendation of a friend or family member who has worked with this advisor before will tell you about the confidence level the advisor inspires in his or her clients. Ideally, you will be meeting with someone who got a rave review from someone you respect.

❏ **Does this advisor seem thorough and detail-oriented?** Is there a process for efficiently gathering your financial information? Expect your advisor to have a sophisticated intake method, either in worksheet form or on the computer. If the "process" is jotting notes on a yellow pad, you might want to think twice about handing over your business.

❏ **Is the response to your financial information nonjudgmental and supportive?** A classic sales approach is to use people's financial weaknesses to push them into purchasing financial products.

("I see you have no disability insurance. Did you know that you are seven times more likely to become sick or disabled than to die in the next ten years? How could you do that to your family? We need to get you into some disability insurance right away.") A true professional will simply make note of the facts, then give recommendations later without recriminations or dramatic flourish. The Trusted Advisor will not make judgements when reviewing your situation. ("Gee, you don't really think this is enough insurance, do you?" "Oh, I can see how, as a novice, you might think. . .")

❏ **Does the advisor take care in reviewing and calculating financial figures?** Although you have been working on gathering your data and will have all of your financial documents organized and ready for review, a competent financial advisor will do his or her own calculating.

❏ **Does this person ask lots of relevant questions and listen well?** In coaching the top echelons of financial advisors, I am constantly reminding them that the way to build trust with clients is not to tell their own stories, but to listen to the clients. The flip side of that is, as a potential client, you should expect to do most of the talking. The advisor should be much more interested in hearing about you—your values, your goals, your financial situation—than in giving you a spiel about his or her experience, superior products, or sales awards.

❑ **Does there seem to be a "fit" between the advisor, the type of clientele the advisor is seeking, the type of advisor you are seeking, and you?** The client-advisor fit is a lot like romantic chemistry: Are you the advisor's ideal client? Is the advisor someone you feel you can trust? Does there seem to be a natural inclination to do business together?

❑ **Does this person fit the profile of a Trusted Advisor?** If you've forgotten the delineation between salespeople and Trusted Advisors, you can refer to pages 96–97. Don't settle. You have already done far more to prepare for your financial plan than most people, and you deserve to work with the best advisor for you.

❑ **Does the administrative support seem sufficient?** A good advisor may be great at the interview and the technical work, but who handles the details and the follow-up? If an advisor is trying to do everything—from correspondence to client contact to answering the phones—this is not a good sign. Trusted Advisors have lives outside the office, take vacations, and are *not* available twenty-four hours a day, seven days a week. Who can provide you with information and assistance when your advisor is not there?

❑ **What do the reports look like and tell you?** Do they focus on performance of specific products (not good) or on your progress toward your overall objectives (excellent)? Do they cover only what the person has sold (not good) or everything in your financial life (excellent)?

CHAPTER 8

TAKE ACTION: STARTING YOUR FINANCIAL FUTURE TODAY

The great end of life is not knowledge but action.

THOMAS HENRY HUXLEY
"Technical Education" (1877)

Taking care of your finances is a lot like raising a child. To be a good parent, you can't just think about the youngster's behavior, understand the principles of child psychology, and consider the benefits of education. Nope, you have to actually guide the child to do what's right, pay attention to his or her feelings, and provide a positive learning environment—and that's not the half of it—some aspects of which last a lifetime.

Likewise, *thinking* about gathering your financial documents, understanding why you need to have investment and spending plans, and *considering* whether you're going to do this yourself or work with a Trusted Advisor will not help you achieve your financial goals and fulfill your values—*unless and until you follow through and take action.*

Getting your financial future planned and getting on that road is one of the most satisfying jobs you'll every undertake. On the other hand, putting it off can be the cause of great regret. In *Charles Kuralt's America,* the beloved journalist eloquently described both the excitement of doing something he'd never done before, and the remorse for not having done other things sooner. Although Mr. Kuralt was writing about his literal travels and not a Financial Road Map, his words are instructive.

> *I planned a trip. I had spent nearly all my life traveling in the United States, but there was one more fanciful journey I had always wanted to make. Now I had the chance, and the prospect thrilled me: I would revisit my favorite American places at just the right time of year—the Florida Keys before it got too hot, the Minnesota canoe country before it got too cold, Charleston in azalea season, Montana in fishing season, Vermont when the oaks and maples turn crimson and gold. I would go to New Orleans and Alaska and the Blue Ridge Mountains and old New Mexico and the coast of Maine. I would go alone . . . and I wouldn't do anything that felt very much like work. I had never been any good at doing nothing; I thought I would try to learn.*
>
> *I would drift with the current of life. I'd be footloose and a little irresponsible, and I'd have a perfect year in America.*

Later in the book, Kuralt wrote about his experience off the coast of Maine while sailing with friends who had twice sailed around the world:

I suffered a pang of envy. I learned to sail when I was still young enough to cross an ocean and promised myself I'd do that someday at the helm of my own boat. But promises postponed have a way of getting broken. Now I was too old, and my ability too rusty, and that particular dream, like so many others, was on the shelf for good.

These passages from Kuralt's wonderful travelogue not only urge us to follow through on our plans, but they also remind us *why* we have plans in the first place: to live out our dreams, to experience the things in life that are exciting and wondrous and memorable.

TAKE THE LONG VIEW

Let's get back to harsh reality for a moment. You are going to die. This is not a scare tactic, just a fact. It's probably going to happen sooner than anybody would like. At some point before then, you will look back on your life and wonder how and why it went by so quickly. You will wish you had done some things less, some things better, some things sooner, some things not at all, and some things more.

When you are eighty or ninety or one hundred years old, you will quite likely look back on your financial history and shake your head in amazement that you were ever hesitant to

- discover your values or determine your goals,
- organize your financial information,
- create a Financial Road Map, and
- do the legwork to competently advise yourself on your own finances, or
- simply hire a Trusted Advisor to do that for you.

If you've already completed all of these tasks, you can look back today and pat yourself on the back. You don't have to wait until you're older. Yet there are still some tasks for you to complete. The remaining steps of financial planning will be the process of determining what has to happen now and over a given period of time to create the future you desire. Looking at your Financial Road Map may put you in a state of excitement, anticipation, or anxiety. Your goals may be entirely achievable given your current income, expenses, and investments. You may already be on track. It's possible, however, that you may have to make some adjustments in your approach. Changes can be made in four areas.

1. You can aspire to different goals. This is my second-least favorite choice since goal reduction can be disheartening and demotivating.

2. You can change your time horizon (target date) for achieving certain goals.

3. You can increase your income. Like gas in a car, money fuels your financial plan so you can go the distance.

4. You can adjust your expenses so you have more money to save and invest, thereby increasing your fuel another way. Some expenses are difficult to adjust because they have become a part of your lifestyle. Others, like taxes, you'd be happy to reduce (legally, of course).

5. You can increase the return on your investments. This is my least favorite choice because the pursuit of higher returns always means increased risk, and we have less control over return on investment than the other options. Of course, it's the one most people like to tackle because it appears to be "easier." It doesn't require any personal

discipline like earning more money or adjusting your expenses. And if it doesn't work, many people shirk responsibility and blame their brokers or money managers. But any belief that you or anyone else can control or predict investment return or performance is an illusion.

There is no magic trick for escaping these simple facts of personal finance, unless you hit a jackpot in Vegas, win the lottery, or have some other windfall. But your Financial Road Map is about financial *planning* and not financial fantasy, and this is where the rubber meets the road. Consider where you are now in each of the Four Quadrants on your Financial Road Map. How much money do you have in cash reserves? Is your insurance sufficient? How much debt are you carrying in relation to your assets? These are now known quantities. What remains is calculating the future, either through your own research or with the help of a professional. Now you've prepared yourself, and the real results will come from going forth and *doing*.

If you are feeling somewhat overwhelmed by the process of taking your financial health to the next level, believe me, I understand. Remember my Ironman training? For the prior ten years, I had stayed in moderate physical condition by running twice a week. And I considered a four- or five-mile run a good workout. Sure, I'd swum a few laps in the pool and ridden a bike. But I had never been a competitive swimmer, cyclist, or runner; I hadn't even participated in those sports in high school or college.

My wife and I were married the same month I started training for the Ironman. In fact, I did my first official Ironman workout, a three-mile jog, on our honeymoon in Kauai. I still didn't really know if I could get through the Ironman. But I really, really wanted to.

And I did do it. On October 3, 1998, I embarked on the most grueling yet gratifying physical test of my life—and survived to tell the tale. No, I didn't win, but I did finish with times in all three components of the event that made me *very happy*.

How did I go from being a moderately fit nonathlete to becoming an Ironman? Yes, coaching from Mark Allen made all the difference, and I couldn't have done it without him. But the linchpin? *Action*.

I worked on my running first, since that was familiar to me, then I added cycling. Next I incorporated weight training to add strength to my growing endurance. By the end of my first month, I was consistently training in these three areas, had educated myself about nutrition, and was applying what I'd learned. On New Year's Day, I added a commitment not to drink any alcohol until after the race.

At times, my task loomed incredibly large, assuming an air of complexity that could be daunting, but it was important for me to keep moving, to keep the confusion from immobilizing me. I felt like giving up sometimes, but I decided that my goal was too important.

GET IN THE POOL

Some of my training was easy, and some of it was hard. One thing I found challenging from the beginning was the swimming component. December passed, then January, and by February I still wasn't swimming. (I had been *thinking* about swimming, however. But thinking and training are not the same thing. The Ironman officials expect you to actually *swim* the 2.4 miles, not stand on the banks and philosophize about it.) I'd heard that 70 percent of being a good swimmer is technique, so I bought the book, *Total Immersion: How to Swim Like a Fish!*

As if thunderstruck by a truly original idea, I said to myself, *Eureka! Fish are great swimmers . . . I have to learn to swim like a fish!*

Next I bought the companion video. I'd *read* in the book about proper stroke technique, and now I *watched* it on video and even *imagined* myself executing perfect strokes. I finally enrolled in the "Total Immersion: Swim Like a Fish!" clinic being held in San Diego during the last weekend of March. I figured I could stay dry till then. No point getting in the water again until I learned the proper technique.

One of the many times Mark gave me invaluable coaching was during this period. In the first week of March, I was helping him with his presentation skills for his motivational speaking career when he asked how my Ironman training was coming. I gave him the full report about my running progress, cycling development, and weight training regimen. I rambled on about my diet and tried to distract him with a few questions, hoping he wouldn't notice I'd left out the swimming part.

But his question was inevitable: "So, how's your swimming going?"

"Um, well . . . ," I stammered. "I've been reading this book and, uh, watching this video about proper technique. And I'm signed up for a swim clinic." I smiled weakly.

His eyes narrowed. "Great. How's it going *in the pool?*"

"Well," I confessed, "I haven't actually been in the pool yet."

"You know, Bill," Mark said slowly and pointedly, "you are going to have to do it. Get. In. The. Pool."

In the end, learning better technique and attending the clinic did make me a better swimmer. In fact, I had wonderful coaches, and my improvement was so significant that I've become something of a poster child for the "Total Immersion" clinic. But only because I finally invested lots of time *in the pool.*

The bottom line is, action equals results. I took the action to bike, run, swim, lift weights, follow a nutrition plan, and listen to my coaches. In just ten months, the result was a twelve-hour, seven-minute, and forty-five-second Ironman finishing time. And no need for medical care after the event.

That's what you have to do now: You must take action. *Get in the pool.* You probably already know exactly what your next steps should be financially, but you may be putting yourself through mental gymnastics to avoid the very things that will take you where you want to go. The sooner you get in the "pool," the sooner you will be on your way to achieving your goals, fulfilling your values, and actualizing your Financial Road Map.

Dr. John Lee introduced me to an invaluable life management concept years ago. He said you can do only one of four things with any activity: do it, delegate it, delay it, or drop it. He called these The Four Ds. Perhaps you've noticed, as I have, that most people take care of financial activities with the third method: delay. Don't be one of the herd! You've come this far; now's your chance to really capitalize on the work you've already done.

No Excuses!

R ose was sixty-one when she told me she had decided to go to law school, which I thought was great. Her son, however, didn't think so. Rose confided, "Andy told me, 'Mom, it'll be four years before you finish law school, and you'll be sixty-five by then.'"

Her reply: "Look, son, how old will I be in four years if I don't go to law school?"

There are no good excuses. Not too old, too poor, too rich, too busy. Failing is never as good as succeeding. Even with a really good excuse.

WHAT DO YOU NEED
TO DO TODAY?

Achieving financial well-being is no small endeavor. Although, as I said at the beginning of this book, money is not that important, living free from financial worry is critical to having a life that excites you, nurtures those you love, and fulfills your highest aspirations.

No doubt different people have different feelings at this point in the book. You may be elated and ready to go: Who knew it could be so simple? Or you may see that you have some work cut out for you but completely understand that it will be worth it. Then again, you may be flat-out frightened.

In every endeavor, there are certain immutable requirements or "natural laws" of success. Yet sometimes, in attempts to avoid discomfort or achieve our goals with less effort or anxiety, we spend too much time and energy hoping to flout those laws. But it cannot, will not, simply does not work. That's why they're called *laws*. Break them and you lose. Surely you recognize that fighting nature is futile. You're not going to receive some special exemption, nor will the financial success gods reveal a secret shortcut.

If you have a future (and all of us do), I suggest you create a Values-Based Financial Road Map and *implement* it. Regardless of whether you are already quite wealthy or are struggling to make ends meet, the basic requirements are the same: You'll have to organize your documents, set goals based on what's important to you, then get whatever coaching or other guidance you need to execute a well-thought-out plan. Simply decide what's next for you, and do it.

My whole purpose in writing this book is to help focus you and then to inspire you to go after your dreams. I will have failed miserably if all you do is turn the last page and say, "That was interesting." The only thing that will make this book a good investment for you is if *you take action*—buffeted by your excitement or despite any fear. This may mean that you have to go back and complete the exercises you skipped. It may mean that you have to get out and start a whole new Do-it-yourselfer's education. It may mean that you simply need to follow the advice of your Trusted Advisor.

You've gotten your feet wet.
Now it's time to get in the pool.
Not next week. Today.

An old English proverb tells us, "One of these days is none of these days." Procrastination can be a terrible thief, robbing you of your energy, focus, and even your dreams. Right now, I suggest you look back over the checklists at the beginning of each of the two sections to see what you have accomplished and what you have yet to complete. Prioritize the remaining items and *get them done!*

Reading about the Values Conversation or goal setting is one way to pass the time; having Values Staircases completed and written on a Financial Road Map, complete with your financial information and milestones, benefits you in ways you can't possibly understand until you do it. And although having a Financial Road Map can feel like a great accomplishment, the real aim is *using* it to create and implement a plan, then staying with it until the job is done. Without action to take this process through to completion, any halfway efforts are all for naught, like planning a vacation but never going.

But if you stay with it—if you complete the exercises, create a plan based on the work you've done, then implement that plan for the rest of your life—you will achieve remarkable things for yourself and those you care most about.

Just get in the pool. Come on in! The water's fine.

ABOUT THE AUTHOR

Bill Bachrach, CSP, is one of the foremost success resources for the financial services industry. His work has been instrumental in helping leaders and producers make the transition from transaction-oriented salespeople to full-service Trusted Advisors.

With a perspective that comes from both having been in the trenches as a salesperson and also having worked with the créme de la créme in the financial services world, Bill is uniquely suited to act as a financial consumers' advocate. His gift is cutting through the hype and the information deluge to get to the heart of what people want most: a financial strategy that fits their values, their goals, and their desired lifestyle.

Bill's industry best-selling book, *Values-Based Selling: The Art of Building High-Trust Client Relationships for Financial Advisors, Insurance Agents and Investment Reps,* is considered by financial professionals to be a "must-read" book about how to serve clients in today's business climate. And *High-Trust Leadership: A Proven System for Developing an Organization of High-Performance Financial Professionals,* its follow-up co-written with insurance sales legend Norman Levine, helps industry leaders understand how best to attract and retain the kind of financial advisors most people want to work with today.

In 1998, Bill achieved a personal milestone by completing the Hawaii Ironman Triathlon. The 2.4-mile swim, 112-mile bike ride, and 26.2-mile marathon run, held every year in the rugged volcanic terrain of Hawaii's Big Island, is considered to be the toughest single-day athletic event in the world.

Bill lives in San Diego with his wife, Anne, who helped him build his business and was vital "support crew" on the training road to Ironman.

D

daVinci, Leonardo, 23 (quoted)
debt, 42, 67, 120, 131
Delegator, xviii, 72, 90
Disney, Roy, 82 (quoted)
Do-it-yourselfer, xviii, 69
Dyer, Wayne, 84

E

E*Trade, 73
Elway, John, 107
emotion, 5, 15, 52
estate plan, 38, 68
evolution of sales, 97
excuses, 135
EXERCISES, CHECKLISTS, AND
    WORKSHEETS
    financial documents checklist,
        36
    Financial Road Map, 50
        (sample)
    Four Quadrants, 40 (sample),
        41
    goals, 27, 30 (samples), 33
    Quality of Life Enhancer, 81, 83
        (sample), 87
    risk management, 46 (sample),
        47
    section 1 checklist, 2
    section 2 checklist, 62
    Trusted Advisor checklist, 124

Values Conversation, 4
Values Staircase, 6 (samples),
    17, 19
"Where I Am Today," 39
expectations, 119
expenses, 130

F

Farmer, Carole, 59 (quoted)
fee-based compensation, 118
financial documents checklist, 36
financial information, 70
    See also media
financial organizer, 121
financial plan, 65, 89
financial planner. *See* advisor, finan-
    cial professional, *and* Trusted
    Advisor
financial "pornography," 65, 72,
    121
financial professional, 38, 49, 52,
    74, 116
Financial Road Map™, xvii, 25, 42,
    49, 65, 86, 93, 129, 137
financial statements, 93, 122
financial strategy, xv, 86, 93
    See also financial plan
financial stress, xvi
following through, 128
Four Quadrants™, 38, 51, 131
Franklin, Benjamin, 82 (quoted)
future value calculation, 57

V

valuation methods, 67

values, xv, xvii, 3, 4 (defined), 26, 89

Values Conversation™, 4, 93, 137
  instructions, 5, 18

Values Staircase™, 6, 29, 51, 58, 137
  levels, 13

Van Dyke, Dick, 24

Vermeil, Dick, 107 (quoted)

W

will, 122

wisdom, 84 (defined), 109

worksheets. *See* EXERCISES, CHECKLISTS, AND WORK-SHEETS

BACHRACH & ASSOCIATES, INC. PRODUCT ORDER FORM

To order call (800) 347-3707, visit our website at
www.ValuesBasedFinancialPlanning.com,
or photocopy this form, and mail to: **Bachrach & Associates, Inc.**
8380 Miramar Mall, Suite 200, San Diego, CA 92121
— or fax to (858) 558-0748. *Thank You!*

ITEM (Volume discounts available on all items—call for details)	QTY	UNIT PRICE	TOTAL
Values-Based Financial Planning Order copies for friends and family!		$29.95	
The Winning Spirit **book** Opening chapter by Bill Bachrach, published in association with the U.S. Olympic Committee		$16.95	
Financial Road Map (22" x 17") Single copy, paper, for desktop use		$ 5.00	
Financial Road Map (22" x 17") Package of 5, paper, for desktop use		$ 9.95	
Financial Road Map (22" x 17") Package of 25, paper, for desktop use		$29.00	
Financial Road Map (39" x 27") Laminated poster for use with dry erasable markers		$99.00	
	SUBTOTAL		
	7.75% SALES TAX (California residents only)		
	SHIPPING (See chart)		
	TOTAL All funds U.S. dollars	$	

U.S. SHIPPING & HANDLING

(call for charges outside U.S. or to expedite shipping):

Orders are shipped UPS GROUND.

For orders
up to $50 — $ 7.00
$51–$100 — $15.00
$101–$300 — $20.00
$301–$600 — $35.00
Over $600
call for price

If you desire express delivery, please call us for assistance. International shipping additional. Does not include customs or brokerage fees.

Revised 3/2002.
Prices subject to change.

BACHRACH
& ASSOCIATES • INC
Values-Based Selling™

❏ **Here's my check** (payable to Bachrach & Associates, Inc.).
Please charge my: ❏ American Express ❏ Visa ❏ MasterCard ❏ Discover

Card # _____ Expires _____

Signature _____

Name _____

Company _____

Address _____

City _____ State _____ Zip _____

Phone (____) _____ Fax (____) _____

e-mail _____

BACHRACH & ASSOCIATES, INC. PRODUCT ORDER FORM

To order call (800) 347-3707, visit our website at
www.ValuesBasedFinancialPlanning.com,
or photocopy this form, and mail to: **Bachrach & Associates, Inc.**
8380 Miramar Mall, Suite 200, San Diego, CA 92121
— or fax to (858) 558-0748. *Thank You!*

ITEM (Volume discounts available on all items—call for details)	QTY	UNIT PRICE	TOTAL
Values-Based Financial Planning Order copies for friends and family!		**$29.95**	
The Winning Spirit **book** Opening chapter by Bill Bachrach, published in association with the U.S. Olympic Committee		**$16.95**	
Financial Road Map (22" x 17") Single copy, paper, for desktop use		**$ 5.00**	
Financial Road Map (22" x 17") Package of 5, paper, for desktop use		**$ 9.95**	
Financial Road Map (22" x 17") Package of 25, paper, for desktop use		**$29.00**	
Financial Road Map (39" x 27") Laminated poster for use with dry erasable markers		**$99.00**	

U.S. SHIPPING & HANDLING

(call for charges outside U.S. or to expedite shipping):

Orders are shipped UPS GROUND.

For orders	
up to $50	$ 7.00
$51–$100	$15.00
$101–$300	$20.00
$301–$600	$35.00
Over $600	call for price

If you desire express delivery, please call us for assistance. International shipping additional. Does not include customs or brokerage fees.

Revised 3/2002.
Prices subject to change.

SUBTOTAL	
7.75% SALES TAX (California residents only)	
SHIPPING (See chart)	
TOTAL All funds U.S. dollars **$**	

BACHRACH
& ASSOCIATES ◆ INC
Values-Based Selling™

❑ **Here's my check** (payable to Bachrach & Associates, Inc.).

Please charge my: ❑ American Express ❑ Visa ❑ MasterCard ❑ Discover

Card # _____ Expires _____

Signature _____

Name _____

Company _____

Address _____

City _____ State _____ Zip _____

Phone (____) _____ Fax (____) _____

e-mail _____

BACHRACH & ASSOCIATES, INC. PRODUCT ORDER FORM

To order call (800) 347-3707, visit our website at
www.ValuesBasedFinancialPlanning.com,
or photocopy this form, and mail to: **Bachrach & Associates, Inc.**
8380 Miramar Mall, Suite 200, San Diego, CA 92121
— or fax to (858) 558-0748. *Thank You!*

ITEM (Volume discounts available on all items—call for details)	QTY	UNIT PRICE	TOTAL
Values-Based Financial Planning Order copies for friends and family!		$29.95	
The Winning Spirit **book** Opening chapter by Bill Bachrach, published in association with the U.S. Olympic Committee		$16.95	
Financial Road Map (22" x 17") Single copy, paper, for desktop use		$ 5.00	
Financial Road Map (22" x 17") Package of 5, paper, for desktop use		$ 9.95	
Financial Road Map (22" x 17") Package of 25, paper, for desktop use		$29.00	
Financial Road Map (39" x 27") Laminated poster for use with dry erasable markers		$99.00	

U.S. SHIPPING & HANDLING
(call for charges outside U.S. or to expedite shipping):
Orders are shipped UPS GROUND.

For orders up to $50	$ 7.00
$51–$100	$15.00
$101–$300	$20.00
$301–$600	$35.00
Over $600	call for price

If you desire express delivery, please call us for assistance. International shipping additional. Does not include customs or brokerage fees.

Revised 3/2002.
Prices subject to change.

SUBTOTAL	
7.75% SALES TAX (California residents only)	
SHIPPING (See chart)	
TOTAL All funds U.S. dollars	$

BACHRACH
& ASSOCIATES • INC
Values-Based Selling™

❑ **Here's my check** (payable to Bachrach & Associates, Inc.).
Please charge my: ❑ American Express ❑ Visa ❑ MasterCard ❑ Discover

Card # _____ Expires _____

Signature _____

Name _____

Company _____

Address _____

City _____ State _____ Zip _____

Phone (_____) _____ Fax (_____) _____

e-mail _____

BACHRACH & ASSOCIATES, INC. PRODUCT ORDER FORM

To order call (800) 347-3707, visit our website at
www.ValuesBasedFinancialPlanning.com,
or photocopy this form, and mail to: **Bachrach & Associates, Inc.**
8380 Miramar Mall, Suite 200, San Diego, CA 92121
— or fax to (858) 558-0748. *Thank You!*

ITEM (Volume discounts available on all items—call for details)	QTY	UNIT PRICE	TOTAL
Values-Based Financial Planning Order copies for friends and family!		**$29.95**	
***The Winning Spirit* book** Opening chapter by Bill Bachrach, published in association with the U.S. Olympic Committee		**$16.95**	
Financial Road Map (22" x 17") Single copy, paper, for desktop use		**$ 5.00**	
Financial Road Map (22" x 17") Package of 5, paper, for desktop use		**$ 9.95**	
Financial Road Map (22" x 17") Package of 25, paper, for desktop use		**$29.00**	
Financial Road Map (39" x 27") Laminated poster for use with dry erasable markers		**$99.00**	

U.S. SHIPPING & HANDLING	

(call for charges outside U.S. or to expedite shipping):

Orders are shipped
UPS GROUND.

For orders
up to $50 $ 7.00
$51–$100 $15.00
$101–$300 $20.00
$301–$600 $35.00

Over $600
call for price

If you desire express delivery, please call us for assistance. International shipping additional. Does not include customs or brokerage fees.

Revised 3/2002.
Prices subject to change.

SUBTOTAL		
7.75% SALES TAX (California residents only)		
SHIPPING (See chart)		
TOTAL All funds U.S. dollars	**$**	

BACHRACH
& ASSOCIATES ◆ INC
Values-Based Selling™

❏ **Here's my check** (payable to Bachrach & Associates, Inc.).
Please charge my: ❏ American Express   ❏ Visa   ❏ MasterCard   ❏ Discover

Card # _____ Expires _____

Signature _____

Name _____

Company _____

Address _____

City _____ State _____ Zip _____

Phone (_____) _____ Fax (_____) _____

e-mail _____

BACHRACH & ASSOCIATES, INC. PRODUCT ORDER FORM

To order call (800) 347-3707, visit our website at
www.ValuesBasedFinancialPlanning.com,
or mail this form to: **Bachrach & Associates, Inc.**
8380 Miramar Mall, Suite 200, San Diego, CA 92121
— or fax to (858) 558-0748. *Thank You!*

ITEM (Volume discounts available on all items—call for details)	QTY	UNIT PRICE	TOTAL
Values-Based Financial Planning Order copies for friends and family!		$29.95	
The Winning Spirit **book** Opening chapter by Bill Bachrach, published in association with the U.S. Olympic Committee		$16.95	
Financial Road Map (22" x 17") Single copy, paper, for desktop use		$ 5.00	
Financial Road Map (22" x 17") Package of 5, paper, for desktop use		$ 9.95	
Financial Road Map (22" x 17") Package of 25, paper, for desktop use		$29.00	
Financial Road Map (39" x 27") Laminated poster for use with dry erasable markers		$99.00	

U.S. SHIPPING & HANDLING

(call for charges outside U.S. or to expedite shipping):

Orders are shipped
UPS GROUND.

For orders
up to $50 $ 7.00
$51–$100 $15.00
$101–$300 $20.00
$301–$600 $35.00
Over $600
call for price

If you desire express delivery, please call us for assistance. International shipping additional. Does not include customs or brokerage fees.

Revised 3/2002.
Prices subject to change.

SUBTOTAL	
7.75% SALES TAX (California residents only)	
SHIPPING (See chart)	
TOTAL All funds U.S. dollars	$

BACHRACH
& ASSOCIATES • INC
Values-Based Selling™

❏ **Here's my check** (payable to Bachrach & Associates, Inc.).
Please charge my: ❏ American Express ❏ Visa ❏ MasterCard ❏ Discover

Card # _____ Expires _____

Signature _____

Name _____

Company _____

Address _____

City _____ State _____ Zip _____

Phone (_____) _____ Fax (_____) _____

e-mail _____

Please fold, seal with tape and drop into any mail box.

NO POSTAGE
NECESSARY
IF MAILED
IN THE
UNITED STATES

Business Reply Mail

First Class Mail Permit No. 23595 San Diego, CA

Postage Will be Paid by Addressee

Bachrach & Associates, Inc.
8380 Miramar Mall, Suite 200
San Diego, CA 92121-9239